NATIONAL DEFENSE RESEARCH INSTITUTE

T0108940

Counterterrorism and Counterinsurgency in Somalia

Assessing the Campaign Against Al Shabaab

Seth G. Jones, Andrew M. Liepman, Nathan Chandler

Prepared for the Office of the Secretary of Defense

Approved for public release; distribution unlimited

For more information on this publication, visit www.rand.org/t/RR1539

Library of Congress Cataloging-in-Publication Data is available for this publication.
ISBN: 978-0-8330-9481-0

Published by the RAND Corporation, Santa Monica, Calif.
© Copyright 2016 RAND Corporation
RAND® is a registered trademark.

Cover: AP Photo/Farah Abdi Warsameh-FILE.

Support RAND
Make a tax-deductible charitable contribution at
www.rand.org/giving/contribute

www.rand.org

Preface

This report analyzes the U.S. and allied campaign against the al Qa'ida–linked terrorist group al Shabaab in Somalia, examines what steps have been most successful against the group, and identifies potential recommendations. The analysis is based on an extensive review of qualitative and quantitative data available on al Shabaab, two trips to East Africa, two trips to U.S. Africa Command, and extensive conversations with regional experts. This study should be of interest to policymakers, academics, and general readers interested in terrorism and insurgency.

This research was conducted within the International Security and Defense Policy Center of the RAND National Defense Research Institute, a federally funded research and development center sponsored by the Office of the Secretary of Defense, the Joint Staff, the Unified Combatant Commands, the Navy, the Marine Corps, the defense agencies, and the defense Intelligence Community.

For more information on the International Security and Defense Policy Center, see www.rand.org/nsrd/ndri/centers/isdp or contact the director (contact information is provided on web page).

Contents

Box, Figures, and Tables

Box

Figures

Tables

Summary

This study examines the counterterrorism and counterinsurgency campaign against al Shabaab in Somalia. It concludes that, while al Shabaab was weakened between 2011 and 2016, the group is by no means defeated and may resurge if urgent steps are not taken to address the political, economic, and governance challenges at the heart of the conflict. In the past year, Somalia has made only halting progress on the political front, the security situation seems to be backsliding, some international donors are tiring, and African Union Mission in Somalia (AMISOM) operations have stagnated. Nevertheless, al Shabaab has lost territory, fighters, finances, popular support, and cohesion. Against the backdrop of this continued threat, Somalia's bloody past, and its history of weak governance, this progress was encouraging.

This study finds that a tailored engagement strategy—which involved deploying a small number of U.S. special operations forces to conduct targeted strikes, provide intelligence, and build the capacity of local partner forces to conduct ground operations—was key in degrading al Shabaab. This strategy used a limited U.S. military footprint, which minimized the risk of U.S. casualties, financial costs, and likelihood of triggering nationalist or religious blowback. It involved working with and supporting the Somali National Army, AMISOM, and clan forces, which were in the lead. There were several other factors that weakened al Shabaab, such as internal friction among al Shabaab's senior cadre caused by poor leadership, battlefield losses, personality clashes, clan dynamics, and ideological disputes.

Still, progress in Somalia is reversible in the absence of continued and consistent pressure and political, economic, and social reforms. Al Shabaab has not given up its ambition to control greater Somalia, and it retains the ability to retake territory, particularly if the United States and its allies fail to effectively deal with the challenges outlined in Chapter Four of this report. In February 2016, al Shabaab fighters retook the Somali port of Merka after AMISOM troops pulled out, underscoring the need for constant vigilance and an armed presence to hold territory that has been cleared. A robust AMISOM force is central to Somalia's ability to prevent al Shabaab's resurgence. Al Shabaab remains a capable and ruthless terrorist group and its intelligence and security branch, Amniyat, remains aggressive in planning future attacks. Al Shabaab continues to kill civilians across East Africa and undermine the viability of Somalia. In June 2016, al Shabaab attacked the Ambassador Hotel in Mogadishu and killed 16 people, including two prominent Somali legislators. The same month, al Shabaab attempted to overrun an AMISOM base near Halgan, which led to the death of 30 Ethiopian soldiers and more than 150 al Shabaab fighters. The pace of attacks increased even as the group lost territory, popular support, finances, and organizational cohesion. It has attacked neighbors, killing hundreds of Kenyans and Ethiopians, and targeted other troop-contributing AMISOM nations.

There remain numerous challenges moving forward. The Somali government and Somali National Army forces remain weak and poorly trained, and AMISOM countries frequently turned to clan militias to help fill the political and security vacuums following al Shabaab's withdrawal. In addition, the United States and other Western governments have not committed enough resources and attention to addressing Somalia's political, economic, and governance challenges at the heart of the conflict. The lack of a permanent U.S. Department of State presence in Somalia contributed to these challenges. Several steps need to occur, such as establishing an on-the-ground U.S. senior diplomatic presence in Somalia to better deal with the country's political challenges; increasing aid to build the institutional capacity of Somali security forces; ensuring long-term political, economic, and military support to AMISOM countries; and retaining the legal authority to deploy U.S. special operations forces and to strike targets in Somalia.

The campaign against al Shabaab also highlights several lessons worth considering for counterterrorism and counterinsurgency operations in other regions. First, tailored engagement is a promising model that bears further examination and refinement. It involves limited direct action by special operations and intelligence forces, assistance to partnered forces that operate in the lead, and diplomatic engagement to ensure that military progress is sustained over the long run. Second, a successful tailored engagement approach requires building the capacity of local partners to retake and hold territory. Territorial control is a *raison d'être* for groups such as al Shabaab, the Islamic State, Jabhat al-Nusra, and al Qa'ida in the Arabian Peninsula. They seek to establish an Islamic emirate, govern populations, attract fighters, and secure finances. The United States and its allies need to focus on building local capacity, which can include supporting the host nation, neighboring states, and legitimate nonstate actors. In Somalia, the United States and its allies helped train, advise, assist, and occasionally accompany AMISOM, Somali National Army forces, and clans to retake and hold territory controlled by al Shabaab. Third, insurgent groups often *increase* terrorist attacks as they lose territory. They may resort to terrorism to coerce the withdrawal of foreign forces by punishing their civilians, bait foreign governments into overreacting, or simply to enact revenge. The lesson for other cases, such as the Islamic State, is straightforward. Western populations should be prepared for an upsurge in violence as groups lose territory.

Today's terrorism and insurgency landscape defies easy solutions, with challenges from the Islamic State, al Qa'ida, and other groups across the Middle East, Europe, Asia, and Africa. While there has been a significant focus on how and why the U.S. and other Western governments have failed to degrade terrorists and insurgents in Iraq, Syria, Afghanistan, Libya, and other countries, there has been far less attention on successful efforts to degrade groups. In Somalia, there has been limited progress. The challenge will be preventing a reversal.

Acknowledgments

We would like to thank those individuals in the U.S. Department of Defense (including U.S. Africa Command, U.S. Special Operations Command, and the Office of the Secretary of Defense), U.S. Department of State, National Security Council, and U.S. Intelligence Community who discussed al Shabaab, Somalia, and East Africa with us in the midst of busy schedules. In particular, the staff at Combined Joint Task Force–Horn of Africa (CJTF-HOA) was extraordinarily helpful in hosting two trips to East Africa and providing outstanding assistance. They were courteous, professional, hardworking, and knowledgeable. We also spoke to government officials from several AMISOM countries, including on trips to East Africa. At the RAND Corporation, Jack Riley was instrumental in helping conceptualize the study and discussing Somalia with CJTF-HOA officials on a trip to Djibouti. Our reviewers, Linda Robinson and Vaughn Bishop, added great value drawn from their deep expertise in insurgency and Africa. Finally, we would like to thank Joy Merck for her outstanding assistance in formatting the document, overseeing the review process, and assisting with publications. She has been a great colleague.

Abbreviations

ACLED	Armed Conflict Location and Event Data Project
AFRICOM	United States Africa Command
AIAI	Al-Itihaad al-Islamiya (early militant group)
AMISOM	African Union Mission in Somalia
ASWJ	Ahlu Suna Waljamaaca
CJTF-HOA	Combined Joint Task Force–Horn of Africa
DoD	U.S. Department of Defense
ICU	Islamic Courts Union
IRA	Irish Republican Army
ISIS	Islamic State of Iraq and al-Sham
ISIL	Islamic State of Iraq and the Levant
NATO	North Atlantic Treaty Organization
NGO	nongovernmental organization
START	National Consortium for the Study of Terrorism and Responses to Terrorism
TFG	Transitional Federal Government
TTP	Tehreek-e-Taliban Pakistan
UN	United Nations
UNITAF	Unified Task Force
UNOSOM	United Nations Operation in Somalia

CHAPTER ONE

Introduction

The study focuses on U.S. and allied efforts against Harakat al Shabaab al-Mujahidin, commonly known as al Shabaab ("the youth"). Beginning in 2006, al Shabaab has waged war in Somalia and neighboring countries to overthrow the Somali government and establish a regime with an extreme version of *sharia*, or Islamic law.[1] Since then, al Shabaab has posed a threat to the United States and other Western governments. Nicholas Rasmussen, director of the National Counterterrorism Center of the U.S. government, noted in 2015 that al Shabaab "continues to threaten U.S. interests in East Africa. We assess it is a potential threat to the Homeland, as some al Shabaab leaders in the past publicly called for transnational attacks, but its interest appears to still be primarily focused on operations in East Africa."[2] In early 2016, director of National Intelligence James Clapper remarked that "Al-Shabaab, al-Qaida's affiliate in East Africa, continues its violent insurgency in southern and central Somalia despite losses of territory and influence and conflict among senior leaders."[3]

---

[1] See, for example, Associated Press, "Final Statement of the Conference of Islamic State Scholars in Somalia," cache of documents found by the Associated Press on the floor in a building occupied by al Qai'da fighters in Timbuktu, Mali, December 3, 2011.

[2] Nicholas J. Rasmussen, "Hearing Before the Senate Select Committee on Intelligence: Current Terrorist Threat to the United States," February 12, 2015, p. 7.

[3] James R. Clapper, "Statement for the Record: Worldwide Threat Assessment of the U.S. Intelligence Community," testimony before the Senate Select Committee on Intelligence, February 9, 2016.

There are several reasons the United States should remain concerned about al Shabaab. First, it possesses a competent external operations capability to conduct attacks outside of Somalia, including against U.S. embassies and other Western targets. Al Shabaab's September 2013 attack at the Westgate Mall in Nairobi, Kenya, and April 2015 attack at Garissa University in heavily Somali-populated North Eastern Province of Kenya demonstrated that the group can plan and conduct attacks across East Africa. Second, al Shabaab officials have expressed an interest in striking U.S. and other foreign targets in East Africa.[4] They have also plotted to kidnap Americans and other foreigners in the region, as well as planned attacks against malls, supermarkets, embassies, and other locations frequented by Westerners.[5] Some al Shabaab members and sympathizers also voiced support for the Islamic State—also known as the Islamic State of Iraq and the Levant (ISIL), Islamic State of Iraq and al-Sham (ISIS), or Daesh—suggesting divisions within al Shabaab about their long-term relationship with al Qa'ida and its affiliates.[6] And some Islamic State fighters in Iraq and Syria reached out to al Shabaab members in Somalia.[7]

Al Shabaab leaders consider the United States and other Western states as enemies and their citizens as *kuffar* (or apostates).[8] As

---

[4]   See, for example, al-Kata'ib Media Foundation, "Punish Them Severely in Order to Disperse Those Who Are Behind Them," 11th episode posted on jihadist websites on July 13, 2015.

[5]   See, for example, "American Officers Killed in a Martyrdom-Seeking Operation on the Outskirts of Mogadishu," Shahada News Agency, March 17, 2014; "An Exclusive Interview with Sheikh Ali Muhammad Hussein, Governor of Islamic Banaadir Province," Shahada News Agency, July 11, 2014; "Ali Dheere: We Targeted the French in Djibouti for Their Massacres in Central Africa," Shahada News Agency, May 27, 2014.

[6]   "IS Fighters and Supporters Celebrate Reports of Possible Pledge from Shaba'ab," SITE Intelligence Group, Western Jihadist Forum Digest, July 13, 2015.

[7]   See, for example, "IS and Supporters Increase Outreach to Shabaab Fighters," SITE Intelligence Group, October 8, 2015.

[8]   "The Experience of Our Brothers in Somalia," in *Al-Qaida Papers*, cache of documents found by the Associated Press on the floor in a building occupied by al-Qai'da fighters in Timbuktu, Mali, undated.

one al Shabaab document noted, it is *halal* (lawful) to kill and rob non-Muslims:

> The French and the English are to be treated equally: Their blood and their money are halal wherever they may be. No Muslim in any part of the world may cooperate with them in any way . . . It leads to apostasy and expulsion from Islam.

The document then added:

> Ethiopians, Kenyans, Ugandans, and Burundians are just like the English and the French because they have invaded the Islamic country of Somalia and launched war on Islam and Muslims.[9]

Al Shabaab has also historically attracted Westerners—including some U.S. citizens in the past—to Somalia. Other foreigners, including from the Somalia diaspora population, have provided financial and other types of support to al Shabaab. Indeed, al Shabaab has attempted to recruit Muslims in the West and other locations.[10] An article titled "From the 'Hood' to an Eternal Paradise" in al Shabaab's magazine *Gaidi Mtaani*, for example, encouraged Americans to move from the streets of U.S. cities to "make Hijra in the path of Allah and take part in the defense and establishment of Islam."[11]

Research Design

In an effort to better understand al Shabaab and U.S. efforts to degrade it, this study asks three sets of questions. First, how have al Shabaab's capabilities evolved over time? Has it grown stronger or weaker? What

---

[9] "The Experience of Our Brothers in Somalia," undated, p. 6.

[10] See, for example, "O Believers, Make Hijra," posted on the Deep Web jihad forum Shumukh al-Islam, August 7, 2015; al-Kata'ib Media Foundation, "From the Frontlines of Honor," posted on jihadist forums on February 2, 2015.

[11] Abu Abdallah al-Muhajir, "From the 'Hood' to an Eternal Paradise," *Gaidi Mtaani*, issue 7, February 2015, pp. 19–24.

are some of the key indicators? Second, what factors have contributed to the evolution of al Shabaab's capabilities? Third, based on answers to these questions, what are key policy recommendations for Somalia? Are there implications for combating other terrorist or insurgent groups?

To answer these questions, this report uses a combination of qualitative and quantitative data. The authors compiled and analyzed hundreds of primary source documents that included the writings, statements, and internal memorandums of al Shabaab leaders. This included such al Shabaab publications as *Gaidi Mtaani* and announcements from organizations such as the Shahada News Agency. The goal was to better understand their objectives and strategies. As political scientists Alexander George and Timothy McKeown argue, it is important to understand

> what stimuli the actors attend to; the decision process that makes use of these stimuli to arrive at decisions; the actual behavior that then occurs; the effect of various institutional arrangements on attention, processing, and behavior; and the effect of other variables of interest on attention, processing, and behavior.[12]

In addition, the authors visited East Africa in January 2015 and July 2015 to discuss the campaign against al Shabaab with military, diplomatic, and intelligence officials from the United States, United Kingdom, Kenya, Uganda, and other countries.

The authors also compiled and analyzed a range of quantitative data, including the number and type of attacks, fatalities, and casualties by al Shabaab. They examined data from several sources, such as the Global Terrorism Database at the National Consortium for the Study of Terrorism and Responses to Terrorism (START), Jane's World Insurgency and Terrorism database, the Armed Conflict Location and Event Data Project (ACLED), and their own estimates.

---

[12] Alexander L. George and Timothy J. McKeown, "Case Studies and Theories of Organizational Decision Making," in Robert F. Coulam and Richard A. Smith, eds., *Advances in Information Processing in Organizations: A Research Annual*, Vol. II (Greenwich, Conn.: JAI Press, 1985), p. 35.

This report frequently refers to *insurgency* and *terrorism*. It defines an *insurgency* as a political and military campaign by a nonstate group (or groups) to overthrow a regime or secede from a country.[13] This definition includes several components. *Insurgent groups* are nonstate organizations, though they may receive assistance from states. They use violence—and the threat of violence—to achieve their objectives. Insurgent groups also have political objectives and seek to govern a specific territory by overthrowing a regime or seceding from a country. Insurgency can be understood, in part, as a process of alternative state building. Groups often tax populations in areas they control, establish justice systems, and attempt to provide other services.[14] *Terrorism*, on the other hand, is a tactic that involves the use of politically motivated violence against noncombatants to cause intimidation or fear among a target audience.[15] Most terrorist groups do not govern territory, although most—if not all—insurgent groups use terrorist tactics against civilians. Consequently, we refer to organizations as insurgent groups when they hold and govern territory.

Since its inception, al Shabaab has been an insurgent group dedicated to reuniting a greater Somalia. This goal requires controlling territory in Somalia and parts of neighboring countries, such as Kenya and Ethiopia, that have Somali populations. But al Shabaab uses terrorism to help achieve its objectives. As this report argues, al Shabaab transformed from an insurgent group that sought to control territory

---

[13] See, for example, the definition of *insurgency* in Central Intelligence Agency, *Guide to the Analysis of Insurgency*, Washington, D.C., 2012, p. 1.

[14] Stathis N. Kalyvas, *The Logic of Violence in Civil War*, New Haven, Conn.: Yale University Press, May 2006, p. 245.

[15] There are many definitions of terrorism. See, for example, U.S. Department of State, *Country Reports on Terrorism 2005*, Washington, D.C., April 2006, p. 9; Bruce Hoffman, *Inside Terrorism*, 2nd edition, New York: Columbia University Press, 2006, pp. 1–41; Robert A. Pape, *Dying to Win: The Strategic Logic of Suicide Terrorism*, New York: Random House, 2005, p. 9; Audrey Kurth Cronin, "Behind the Curve: Globalization and International Terrorism," *International Security*, Vol. 27, No. 3, Winter 2002/2003, p. 33.

and govern its inhabitants to one that controlled little territory and increasingly relied on terrorist attacks.[16]

Outline of the Report

The rest of this report is divided into several chapters. Chapter Two examines how al Shabaab's goals and capabilities have evolved over time. Chapter Three analyzes the factors that contributed to the weakening of al Shabaab, including African Union Mission in Somalia (AMISOM) military operations, U.S. and other Western engagement, and other factors within Somalia. Chapter Four examines key challenges facing the campaign against al Shabaab, along with recommendations for Somalia for U.S. and Western efforts globally.

---

[16] Somalia also is a case that defies definitions. For much of the period covered in this report, Somalia lacked any semblance of a central government, and thus al Shabaab and its antecedents were one of many groups vying to grab power within the governance vacuum. As its fortunes waned, al Shabaab transitioned from an insurgent organization whose principal aim was to control territory to one that shifted its emphasis to mass-casualty terrorist attacks.

CHAPTER TWO

The Evolution of al Shabaab

This chapter examines al Shabaab's historical evolution. It is organized into five chronological periods: (1) ideological and historical origins (1960s–2005), (2) proto-insurgent phase (2005–2007), (3) rebirth and rise to organizational maturity (2007–2009), (4) the peak of its territorial control and institutional power (2009–2011), and (5) weakening and devolution to a terrorist group (2011–2016). Each of these sections examines qualitative and quantitative trends using a range of proxies for al Shabaab strength, such as the number of fighters, number of attacks, territorial control, and organizational cohesion. It also notes, where possible, information on popular support for al Shabaab and group finances.

The chapter finds that al Shabaab's political and military fortunes as well as the extent of local support it has enjoyed have varied considerably over time. The group experienced an increase in the number of fighters, number of attacks, organizational cohesion, and territorial control through 2010. Beginning in 2011, however, al Shabaab's strength began to wane. By 2016, it had lost fighters, substantial territory, and cohesion. Nevertheless, despite its military and political setbacks, it was able to conduct more terrorist attacks. The next chapter builds on these findings and examines why al Shabaab weakened by 2016. Table 2.1 provides a summary of selected indicators.

Table 2.1
Selected Indicators of al Shabaab's Strength

Years	Range of Fighters	Number of Terrorist Attacks and Civilian Casualties[a]	Organizational Cohesion	Al Shabaab's Approximate Areas of Influence (on Percentage of Somali Population)[b]
Phase 1: 1960s–2005	0–30	2 attacks (Average: less than 1 per month) 3 killed (Average: less than 1 per month)	Low	0 percent
Phase 2: 2005–2006	30–400	4 attacks (Average: less than 1 per month) 20 killed (Average: less than 1 per month)	Moderate	10 percent (as of fall 2006)
Phase 3: 2007–2009	1,000–7000	59 attacks (Average: 2 per month) 286 killed (Average: 12 per month)	Moderate	35 percent (as of fall 2008)
Phase 4: 2009–2011	5,000–12,000	135 attacks (Average: 6 per month) 364 killed (Average: 15 per month)	Moderate	55 percent (as of spring 2010)
Phase 5: 2011–2016	3,000–8,000	1,962 attacks (Average: 33 per month) 4,233 killed (Average: 71 per month)	Low	5 percent (as of summer 2016)

NOTES: Data are from the STARTGlobal Terrorism Database; Jane's World Insurgency and Terrorism database; ACLED; U.S. Department of State, *Country Reports on Terrorism*, various years; Stig Jarle Hansen, *Al-Shabaab in Somalia: The History of a Militant Islamist Group, 2005–2012*, New York: Oxford University Press, 2013; Rob Wise, "Al-Shabaab," AQAM Future Project Case Studies Report, Washington, D.C.: Center for Strategic and International Studies, July 2011; Ken Menkhaus, "Al-Shabab's Capabilities Post-Westgate," *CTC Sentinel*, March 24, 2014; United Nations (UN), *Population Estimation Survey 2014: For the 18 Pre-War Regions of Somalia*, October 2014; author estimates.

[a] Excludes 2016 data, which were not yet available at time of publication. Additionally, START does not attribute any attack to al Shabaab before 2007. The open-source data presented here on number of attacks and casualties underrepresents the actual figures due to several factors. One reason is that

Table 2.1—Continued

many attacks that take place in Somalia go unclaimed by the perpetrators. This is particularly true in the earlier years of al Shabaab's existence, before it had developed sophisticated media and Internet operations. In 2007, for instance, START researchers coded 151 attacks in Somalia, but attributed only 21 to al Shabaab. The remaining 86 percent of attacks in 2007 were attributed to "unknown" perpetrators, even though many if not all were likely committed by al Shabaab. Similarly, in 2008, al Shabaab was credited with 38 attacks compared with 129 attacks attributed to "unknown" perpetrators. Another reason for underreporting is that open-source news reports often describe casualties in vague terms, such as "several" or "dozens" or "hundreds" killed or wounded. In such cases, START researchers have adopted a conservative coding methodology (see START Codebook for details). Nevertheless, *the trends* presented in these data are believed to accurately reflect al Shabaab's activities.

[b] Area of influence estimates are RAND calculations based on demographic data published in UN, October 2014, p. 31. Phase two is based on the population of Mogadishu (approximately 1.23 million); phase three is based on the population of Lower Shabelle, Bay, Bakool, Lower Juba, Middle Juba, and Mogadishu (approximately 4.49 million); phase four is based on the population of Galgaduud, Hiraan, Middle Shabelle, Lower Shabelle, Bay, Bakool, Gedo, Middle Juba, and Lower Juba (approximately 6.98 million); phase five is based on portions of the rural and nomadic population of Lower Juba, Middle Juba, Lower Shabelle, and Bay (approximately 0.6 million).

Phase One: Ideological and Historical Origins, 1960s–2005

Al Shabaab's ideological origins can be traced to the 1960s, when Salafi and Wahhabi networks from Saudi Arabia and Egypt were first introduced into Somalia, challenging the Sufi Koranic supporters who had historically dominated. Somalia's first generation of modern jihadists went to Afghanistan in the early 1980s to join the *mujahideen* against Soviet forces. These fighters—many of whom would later become founders and leaders of al Shabaab—eventually returned to Somalia and attempted to spread into Somalia a pan-Islamist ideology inspired by such individuals as Abdullah Azzam.[1] Al-Itihaad al-Islamiya (AIAI), an early militant group that would eventually contribute to the ranks of al Shabaab, was founded in Somalia in 1983. It aimed to overthrow Siad Barre's regime and establish an Islamic state in the region, includ-

---

[1] On the influence of Azzam on foreign fighters, see, for example, Thomas Hegghammer, "The Rise of Muslim Foreign Fighters: Islam and the Globalization of Jihad," *International Security*, Vol. 35, No. 3, Winter 2010/2011, pp. 53–94.

ing in Somalia and parts of Kenya, Ethiopia, and Djibouti.[2] In January 1991, Siad Barre's regime collapsed after two decades in power. The ensuing years were marked by governance weakness, interclan warfare, and warlord control over much of Somalia. In this chaos, AIAI emerged as one of the most powerful insurgent groups. The radical views of the first generation of Afghan veterans impressed many young AIAI members, including future al Shabaab leaders Aden Hashi Ayro and Mukhtar Robow.[3] From 1992 to 1995, U.S. and other international forces operating under UN auspices—including the United Nations Operation in Somalia I (UNOSOM I), Unified Task Force (UNITAF), and UNOSOM II—deployed to Somalia to help monitor a cease-fire in Mogadishu, escort deliveries of humanitarian aid, and ultimately establish a secure environment in Somalia.[4]

The deployment of U.S. forces to Somalia was a catalytic event for al Qa'ida leaders, who issued a fatwa from Khartoum and alleged that the U.S. objective was to dominate the Persian Gulf and the Horn of Africa. Osama bin Laden also set up a cell in Nairobi and used it to send weapons and trainers to Somali warlords battling U.S. forces.[5] After U.S. and UN forces withdrew from Somalia in 1995, AIAI activities expanded, particularly against Ethiopian targets. These advances, however, were short lived. Beginning in 1996, Ethiopian forces and clan militias held a series of military operations, and AIAI suffered from internal splintering over ideological and strategic differences.

Three important developments occurred around this time. First, a second generation of Somali Salafi–jihadists—such as Aden Hashi

---

[2] Daveed Gartenstein-Ross, "The Strategic Challenge of Somalia's Al-Shabaab: Dimensions of Jihad," *Middle East Quarterly*, Vol. 16, No. 4, Fall 2009, pp. 25–36.

[3] Hansen, 2013, pp. 20–21.

[4] UN, *The Blue Helmets: A Review of United Nations Peace-keeping*, 3rd ed., New York: UN Department of Public Information, 1996; Walter Clarke and Jeffrey Herbst, *Learning from Somalia: The Lessons of Armed Humanitarian Intervention*, Boulder, Colo.: Westview Press, 1997.

[5] On the al Qa'ida reaction, see National Commission on Terrorist Attacks upon the United States, *The 9/11 Commission Report*, New York: W. W. Norton, 2004, pp. 59–60; Daniel Benjamin and Steven Simon, *The Age of Sacred Terror: Radical Islam's War Against America*, New York: Random House, 2003, pp. 118–123.

Farah Ayro—traveled to Afghanistan to undergo training during the Taliban reign. Some trained in al Qa'ida camps in eastern and southern Afghanistan. Second, Somali warlords and clan leaders who controlled Somalia for much of the decade became even more fragmented, and Somalia itself decentralized further. In northeastern Somalia, Puntland leaders declared the area an autonomous state in 1998. In northwestern Somalia, Somaliland had already become an autonomous region in 1991, which was affirmed in a referendum held in 2001. Third, the so-called Sharia Courts, which consisted of nearly a dozen clan-based, independently established ad hoc courts that implemented justice in Mogadishu and other areas, merged together to form the Islamic Courts Union (ICU). Its goal was to form an Islamic community to unify the country under Islam, rather than clan allegiance. The ICU targeted a number of clans, banned films it deemed inappropriate, and tackled major crimes. Although the ICU claimed to be a unifying organization that valued Islam over clan allegiance and was initially seen by many as a viable alternative to the chaos it supplanted, the Hawiye clan ruled ten of the 11 courts.[6] The ICU welcomed many first- and second-generation Afghanistan veterans—including former AIAI and future al Shabaab members—who secured leadership positions.[7]

In 2001 and 2002, more than a hundred Somalis traveled to Afghanistan to fight alongside al Qa'ida and the Taliban, including future al Shabaab leaders Aden Hashi Ayro, Mukhtar Robow, Ahmed Godane, Abdullah Salad, and Ibrahim Haji Jama al-Afghani. In addition, al Qa'ida operatives in East Africa recruited more local Somalis.[8] Following the United States–led overthrow of the Taliban, many of the operatives who were not killed or captured returned to Somalia as the United States conducted a low-level counterterrorism campaign.

---

[6] BBC News, "Profile: Somalia's Islamic Courts," June 6, 2006.

[7] Hansen, 2013, pp. 19–29.

[8] In what arguably proved a turning point that would spur greater U.S. counterterrorism resources flowing to Somalia, on November 28, 2002, Somali and Kenyan members of al Qa'ida in East Africa shot down an Israeli airliner in coordination with a suicide attack on the Israeli-owned Paradise Hotel in Mombasa. Future al Shabaab leaders Saleh Ali Saleh Nahban, Fadil Harun (aka Fazul Abdullah Mohammed), and Abu Talha al-Sudani were involved in planning the high-profile, mass-casualty operation.

The United States cooperated with faction leaders, former military and police officers, and the security services in Somaliland and neighboring Puntland to locate and kill or capture operatives linked to al Qa'ida.[9] Still, the governance vacuum in Somalia provided an opportunity for jihadist groups to thrive.[10]

Phase Two: Proto-Insurgency, 2005–2007

By the beginning of 2005, the organizations that eventually became al Shabaab formed a loose network of approximately 30 core members that included Afghan veterans, former AIAI members, and remnants of al Qa'ida in East Africa.[11] Mukhtar Robow claimed that a key impetus for the creation of al Shabaab around 2005 was the need for better unification among these extremists:

> Al Shabaab was formed not too long ago after people returned from the fighting in Afghanistan in which the Taliban was ousted. Some officials of the Islamic movements who were in the country at the time held a meeting having felt that their groups were not that active as far jihad was concerned. There were various Somali Islamic movements that have in the past tried to carry out jihad but they were faced with many obstacles and dropped their operations altogether. The men who were previously in these groups held a meeting and decided to form a movement and take part in the jihad and spread the religion.[12]

---

[9] International Crisis Group, *Counter-Terrorism in Somalia: Losing Hearts and Minds*, Africa Report No. 95, Brussels, Belgium: International Crisis Group, July 2005; International Crisis Group, *Somalia's Islamists*, Africa Report No. 100, Brussels, Belgium: International Crisis Group, 2005.

[10] Ken Menkhaus, *Somalia: State Collapse and the Threat of Terrorism*, Adelphi Paper 364, New York: Oxford University Press, 2005.

[11] Hansen, 2013, pp. 28–32.

[12] "Al Jazeera Interview with Al-Shabab Spokesman," BBC, March 7, 2009.

In June 2006, the ICU took power in Somalia, overcoming a U.S.-backed group of mostly secular warlords, the Alliance for the Restoration of Peace and Counter-Terrorism.[13] In August 2006, al Shabaab formally announced its establishment as a splinter group of the ICU.[14] By this time, al Shabaab included a growing force of several hundred fighters, and its leaders were present in the ICU militias, which now controlled Mogadishu. Mukhtar Robow, who hailed from the Rahanwhein clan, was a rising star and eventually became second in command of the ICU security forces. Ahmed Godane was appointed secretary general in the executive council of the ICU, Fuad Mohamed Khalaf Shongole was responsible for education and youth in the executive council, and Myhedin Mohamed Omar held the cabinet position overseeing health affairs. Al Shabaab held nine of 97 seats in the Shura Council, and it received sizable funding from the courts. In September 2006, al Shabaab and ICU forces seized control of the port city of Kismayo, a strategic location that served as the commercial capital of Jubaland and became one of al Shabaab's principal sources of funding.[15]

On December 6, 2006, Ethiopia invaded Somalia to fight the ICU and other militia forces, and Ethiopian forces entered Mogadishu with little opposition. As the next section highlights, the invasion triggered a significant anti-Ethiopian backlash among Somalis inside and outside the country. Salafi-jihadist groups such as al Qa'ida also used the invasion as an opportunity to recruit fighters. Ethiopian forces, supported by U.S. military forces, targeted ICU and al Shabaab forces over the course of December 2006. On December 28, 2006,[16] the Transitional Federal Government (TFG) reentered Mogadishu for the first time since its founding in exile and, in January 2007, Kismayo

---

[13] See, for example, Abdel Bari Atwan, *After bin Laden: Al Qaeda, The Next Generation*, New York: The New Press, 2012, p. 113.

[14] Somaliland Times, "Extremist Splinter Group of Somali Islamic Courts Formed," August 12, 2006.

[15] Hansen, 2013, pp. 35–36.

[16] Gartenstein-Ross, 2009, pp. 25–36; Michael R. Gordon and Mark Mazetti, "U.S. Used Base in Ethiopia to Hunt Al Qaeda," *New York Times*, February 23, 2007.

fell quickly to Ethiopian and TFG forces. In January 2007, AMISOM forces also entered the country to maintain peace in Mogadishu.[17]

Phase Three: Rebirth and the Rise of the Islamists, 2007–2009

At the start of 2007, al Shabaab's future was uncertain. Many of its top leaders were dead, and its remaining forces were demoralized and defeated. The leadership of al Shabaab was internally unified but in conflict with the remnants of ICU, which had traditionally been an important source of funding and recruitment for al Shabaab. Ethiopian forces, which numbered about 5,000 soldiers, controlled most of southern Somalia. In addition, AMISOM, consisting of several thousand Ugandan and Burundian troops, deployed to Mogadishu in February 2007 to support the TFG.

Led by veterans Godane, Afghani, and Shongole, al Shabaab focused on strengthening its organizational structure and rearming its ranks in southern Somalia. The organization also established an Internet presence, initially directing its messaging toward a domestic audience. But it soon expanded its online propaganda and recruiting efforts overseas. The Somali diaspora community became an increasingly important source of funds and recruits beginning around 2007. According to some estimates, the Somali diaspora population sent more than $1 billion in remittances back to the country annually.[18] Although it is unclear how much of these financial flows reached al Shabaab's coffers, it was likely significant in al Shabaab's early years. Additionally, the organization's increasing alignment with al Qa'ida helped al Shabaab solicit funding from wealthy Arab backers.[19]

Al Shabaab's recruitment efforts were bolstered in 2007 by clan divisions, widespread opposition to Ethiopian forces, and an increasingly illegitimate TFG, whose police forces were widely viewed as pred-

---

[17] Wise, 2011.

[18] Menkhaus, 2014.

[19] Wise, 2011.

atory. With no central government to provide law and order, al Shabaab appeared capable of filling the vacuum. Al Shabaab took advantage of a surge in nationalism in 2007 and 2008 as foreign fighters flocked to Somalia to oppose Ethiopian occupation. Around this time, Americans from cities like Phoenix and Minneapolis began to travel to Somalia to fight with al Shabaab.[20] Between 2007 and 2010, more than 40 Americans traveled to Somalia to join al Shabaab, making the United States a primary exporter of Western fighters to Somalia.[21] Al Shabaab made an active attempt to recruit young American men both in person and on the Internet. Some of the initial recruiters had participated in earlier rounds of fighting in Somalia and returned to the United States as veterans with tantalizing war stories.[22] In addition to Minneapolis, Minnesota, and Phoenix, Arizona, al Shabaab recruiters attempted to attract recruits in other American cities such Boston, Massachusetts; Seattle, Washington; San Diego, California; Washington, D.C.; Columbus, Ohio; and Lewiston, Maine.[23]

During the spring and summer of 2007, al Shabaab remained on the margins of the war between Ethiopian and TFG forces on one side, and clan-based militias on the other.[24] By the fall of 2007, al Shabaab began to resurge. It severed its alliance with the ICU, its ranks swelled with refugees from Mogadishu, its forces were well organized and well paid, its operational tempo increased, and its local popularity was

---

[20] U.S. Department of State, Office of the Coordinator for Counterterrorism, "Designation of al-Shabaab," March 18, 2008.

[21] Committee on Homeland Security, *Al Shabaab: Recruitment and Radicalization Within the Muslim American Community and the Threat to the Homeland*, Washington, D.C., Government Printing Office, July 27, 2011, p. 2.

[22] Brian Michael Jenkins, *Stray Dogs and Virtual Armies: Radicalization and Recruitment to Jihadist Terrorism in the United States Since 9/11*, Santa Monica, Calif.: RAND Corporation, OP-343-RC, 2011, pp. 12–14.

[23] United States District Court, District of New Jersey, *United States of America v. Mohamed Alessa and Carlos E. Almonte*, Magistrate No.: 10-8109 (MCA), June 4, 2010; United States District Court for the Eastern District of Virginia, Alexandria Division, *United States of America v. Zachary Adam Chesser*, Position of the United States with Respect to Sentencing Factors, Case 1:10-cr-00395-LO, Document 46, February 18, 2011.

[24] Al Shabaab launched its first major wave of suicide attacks in March–April 2007.

buoyed by the group's perceived ability to enact justice and resolve clan differences. In December 2007, al Shabaab announced that Godane was its new leader, and the U.S. Department of State eventually designated the group as a foreign terrorist organization in 2008.[25] As Figure 2.1 highlights, al Shabaab increased its freedom of movement over the course of 2008 and into early 2009.[26]

In August 2008, al Shabaab and allied forces from the Ras Kamboni clan captured Kismayo from the Marehan clan, which had controlled the city since shortly after the Ethiopian invasion. Over the next several months, al Shabaab forces advanced northward from Kismayo to Mogadishu, winning limited victories against Ethiopian forces in coastal areas such as Merka, Qoreole, and Baraawe. Northwest of Mogadishu, al Shabaab forces faced Somali government and Ethiopian offensives in towns such as Bardale, Ufurow, Buurhakaba, Qansah-Dheere, Wajid, and Huddur in the districts of Bay and Bakool.[27] During these engagements, al Shabaab adopted a guerrilla strategy using military and political resources to mobilize the Somali population, conduct hit-and-run attacks, and undermine the government's will to fight.[28] In November 2008, the city of Merka—just 60 kilometers south of Mogadishu—fell to al Shabaab fighters.

---

[25] U.S. Department of State, 2008.

[26] *Area of influence* is defined as territory where al Shabaab had freedom of movement. Its fighters did not necessarily control local populations in these areas directly using al Shabaab security forces, but al Shabaab members could freely move around during the day and night with little fear of capture by local or government forces.

[27] Hansen, 2013, pp. 69–71.

[28] On guerrilla strategies, see Mao Tse-Tung, *On Guerrilla Warfare*, Urbana and Chicago, Ill.: University of Illinois Press, 2000; Walter Laqueur, *Guerrilla Warfare: A Historical and Critical Study*, New Brunswick, N.J.: Transaction Publishers, 2010; John Shy and Thomas W. Collier, "Revolution War," in Peter Paret, ed., *Makers of Modern Strategy: From Machiavelli to the Nuclear Age*, Princeton, N.J.: Princeton University Press, 1986, pp. 815–862; Gérard Chaliand, ed., *Guerrilla Strategies: An Historical Anthology from the Long March to Afghanistan*, Berkeley, Calif.: University of California Press, 1982.

Figure 2.1
Al Shabaab Freedom of Movement, Late 2008

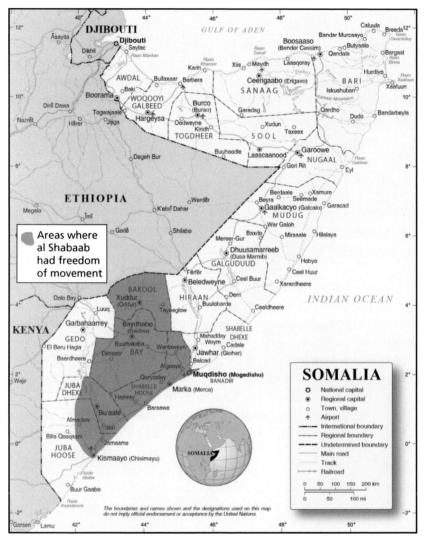

NOTE: Data are from AMISOM; the START database; Jane's World Insurgency and
Terrorism database; Hansen, 2013; AFRICOM; and author estimates.
RAND RR1539-2.1

Phase Four: The Heyday of al Shabaab, 2009–2011

Al Shabaab's territorial control expanded swiftly following the Ethiopian withdrawal in 2009. Al Shabaab took Baidoa, the interim capital of the TFG, on January 26, 2009, and seized territory north and west of Mogadishu in areas such as Jowhar, Beled Weyne, Hudur, Hiraan, and Bakool. In October, al Shabaab took over control of Kismayo, displacing the Ras Kamboni clan and taking over the lucrative charcoal trade and other activities at the port. In the spring and summer of 2010, al Shabaab continued its expansion by capturing territory from Ahlu Sunna Wah Jamaa (ASWJ), a paramilitary group that consisted of moderate Sufis and fighters from the Hawadle, Ayr, Abgal-Waisle, and other clans.[29] In December 2010, al Shabaab took control of the pirate port city of Haradere—an important revenue source—after defeating and incorporating Hizbul Islam. By some estimates, al Shabaab was able to generate at least $1 million per day through taxation at the ports and at checkpoints.

Around this time, al Shabaab also began to conduct limited, cross-border raids into Kenya with increasing frequency. This period marked a rise in al Shabaab's operations beyond Somalia's borders. Al Shabaab declared jihad against Kenya because of its support for the Somali government. Leader Ahmed Godane announced the group's intention to merge with al Qa'ida, pledging "to connect the horn of Africa jihad to the one led by al Qa'ida and its leader Sheikh Osama bin Laden."[30]

As Figure 2.2 illustrates, by 2010, al Shabaab had freedom of movement in most of southern Somalia. It was an area the size of Denmark, with about 5 million inhabitants, which made up about 50 percent of Somalia's total population.[31] Despite al Shabaab's vast territorial

---

[29] Hansen, 2013, pp. 73–102.

[30] Al Shabaab, Public Statement, February 1, 2010. Also see, for example, Sarah Childress, "Somalia's Al Shabaab to Ally with Al Qaeda," *Wall Street Journal*, February 2, 2010.

[31] The estimate on al Shabaab's control of territory comes from Hansen, 2013, p. 72. Somalia's population in 2009 was approximately 9.38 million. World Bank, "Data: Somalia," undated.

Figure 2.2
Al Shabaab Freedom of Movement, Late 2010

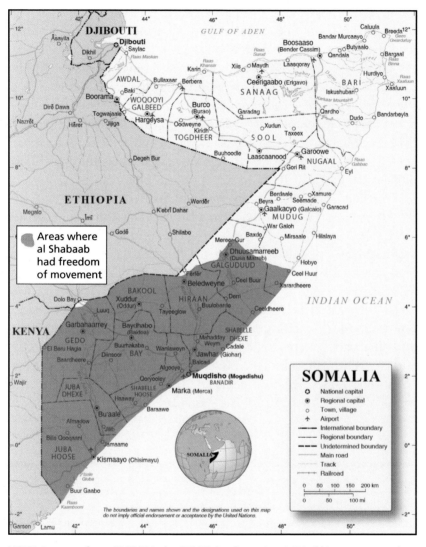

NOTE: Data are from AMISOM; the START database; Jane's World Insurgency and Terrorism database; Hansen, 2013; AFRICOM; and author estimates.

RAND RR1539-2.2

control, its full-time membership numbered only about 5,000.[32] Consequently, it often failed to adequately govern territory under its control, it brought in new recruits who were not always committed to its long-term objectives, and leadership fissures began to emerge. In addition, al Shabaab also engaged in repeated conflicts with armed groups, including clan militias and ASWJ.[33]

On July 9, 2010, al Shabaab issued a statement encouraging foreign jihadists to attack Ugandan and Burundian embassies worldwide in retaliation for their participation in AMISOM.[34] Two days later, in its first major attack outside of Somalia, al Shabaab suicide bombers killed 76 civilians watching a World Cup match at a cafe in Kampala, Uganda. In response, the African Union agreed to expand AMISOM's mandate on July 22, 2010, from a peacekeeping to a peace-enforcement mission, allowing units to engage al Shabaab directly.[35]

On August 23, 2010, al Shabaab launched its Ramadan offensive, named *Nahayatu Muxtadiin* (or "end of the apostates"), with spectacular, coordinated suicide attacks on the Presidential Palace and Muna Hotel in Mogadishu, which killed more than 100 TFG politicians and civil servants, including six parliamentarians. Over the next several weeks, however, al Shabaab suffered a series of defeats, described in more detail in Chapter Three. By mid-September, an estimated 500 to 700 al Shabaab fighters—including many top leaders—were killed, and another 2,000 were wounded. Taken together, more than 25 percent of al Shabaab's forces had been depleted. The operation also drained the group's coffers.[36] The failure of the Ramadan offensive also exacerbated

---

[32] Hansen, 2013, p. 83.

[33] On local perceptions of al Shabaab, see Andrea Levy, *Looking Toward the Future: Citizen Attitudes about Peace, Governance, and the Future in Somalia*, Washington, D.C.: National Democratic Institute for International Affairs, December 2010; Andrea Levy, *Searching for Peace: Views and Comments from Somalia on the Foundations of a New Government*, Washington, D.C.: National Democratic Institute for International Affairs, September 2011.

[34] Al Shabaab, public statement, July 9, 2010. Also see, for example, "Somalia's Shabab Calls on Global Islamist Militants to Attack Ugandan and Burundian Targets," *Jane's Terrorism and Insurgency Centre*, July 9, 2010.

[35] Wise, 2011.

[36] Hansen, 2013, pp. 100–102.

rivalries within the al Shabaab leadership ranks, particularly between Ahmed Abdi Godane on the one hand and Mukhtar Robow, Fuad Khalaf Shongole, and Hassan Yaqubi on the other.[37]

One of the main proponents of the Ramadan offensive, Godane, came under withering criticism from al Shabaab commanders such as Yaqubi, Shongole, and Robow for shifting away from hit-and-run guerrilla attacks and to more-conventional operations.[38] After the offensive, al Shabaab's Shura council fractured. Anger within the organization was directed at Godane, along with subcommanders, such as Robow, for withdrawing from combat too quickly.[39] As battlefield losses mounted, additional fissures opened within the organization. Osama bin Laden and al Qa'ida operative Fazul Abdullah Mohammed criticized al Shabaab and Godane for causing civilian casualties and unnecessarily killing Muslims.[40]

Phase Five: Retreat and Adaptation, 2011–2016

Between February and May 2011, AMISOM launched multiple offensives against al Shabaab strongholds throughout Mogadishu, described in more detail in Chapter Three. By early 2011, AMISOM had gained control of 13 of the capital's 16 districts, including key revenue sources such as the Bakara market.

Beyond Mogadishu, al Shabaab forces were stretched thin across multiple fronts in the spring of 2011, and they suffered territorial losses in Gedo to Somali militias supported by Kenya and Ethiopia. By the

---

[37] Stig Jarle Hansen, "An In-Depth Look at Al-Shabab's Internal Divisions," *CTC Sentinel*, Vol. 7, No. 2, February 2014, pp. 9–12.

[38] Hansen, 2013, pp. 101–104.

[39] Mohamed Shil, "Al-Shabab: What Will Happen Next?" *Somalia Report*, September 3, 2011.

[40] Nelly Lahoud, *Beware of Imitators: Al-Qa'ida Through the Lens of Its Confidential Secretary*, West Point, N.Y.: Harmony Program at the Combating Terrorism Center at West Point, 2012; Nelly Lahoud, Stuart Caudill, Liam Collins, Gabriel Koehler-Derrick, Don Rassler, and Muhammad al-'Ubaydi, *Letters from Abbottabad: Bin Ladin Sidelined?* West Point, N.Y.: Harmony Program at the Combating Terrorism Center at West Point, 2012.

Table 2.2
Average Lethality by al Shabaab Attack Type, 2008–2015

Tactic	Frequency of Attacks	Total Confirmed Killed (Including Insurgents)	Average Lethality per Attack
Ambushes and raids[a]	676	1,894	2.8
Bombings/explosions	737	2,062	2.8
Suicide attacks[b]	98	1,093	11.2
Assassinations[c]	172	291	1.7
Kidnappings[d]	229	2,937 (kidnappings)	12.8 (kidnappings per incident)
Sabotage attacks[e]	39	25	0.6
Unknown tactic	299	889	3.0

NOTE: The data are from the START Global Terrorism Database (GTD).

[a] The START database labels ambushes and raids as "armed/unarmed assaults."

[b] In the START database, suicide attacks are coded as a subtype, and they can come from multiple categories, namely bombings and assassinations.

[c] The START database does not have data on mutilations.

[d] We used the number of hostages taken, rather than the number killed, since most insurgent groups release hostages in exchange for money or prisoners.

[e] The START database labels sabotage operations as "facility/infrastructure sabotage." In addition, it does not have data on other subversive acts.

start of the historic East African drought in July 2011, al Shabaab was on the retreat in Mogadishu and on tenuous ground in many areas of the south. Recruiting had slowed, in part because foreign fighters left to participate in the Arab uprisings; the organization's financial situation was in trouble; and violent interfactional clashes erupted within the group. By August 2011, al Shabaab announced that it had withdrawn all of its militants from Mogadishu.[41] Beginning in the summer of 2011, al Shabaab launched a new wave of suicide attacks, assassinations, roadside improvised explosive devices, and small hit-and-run ambushes. As shown in Table 2.2, suicide attacks have been al Shabaab's most lethal tactic, averaging more than 11 deaths per attempt

---

[41] Sheikh Ali Muhammed Rage, public statement, Shabelle Media Network, August 6, 2011.

since 2008. Al Shabaab had benefited from its control of commercial activity in Bakara market, Mogadishu's main bazaar. But this income was severely curtailed in 2011, when al Shabaab lost control of the city.[42]

On October 14, 2011, Kenya launched a combined air and ground offensive (Operation Linda Nchi) in the Jubbada Hoose region south of Mogadishu, marking the start of another phase of important territorial losses for al Shabaab. Assisted by TFG and clan militia forces, Kenyan forces assaulted al Shabaab positions in Ras Kamboni, Kismayo, Baidoa, Afgoye, and elsewhere in southern Somalia throughout the fall/winter of 2011 and into 2012.

In January 2012, al Shabaab announced that it would expand operations in Kenya, in part a result of Kenya's military intervention in Somalia. It increased terrorist attacks on soft targets in Kenya, including police stations, churches, bus stops, bars, and refugee camps.[43] In February 2012, Godane declared the group's formal merger with al Qa'ida, making good on his promise announced two years before.[44] Meanwhile, AMISOM's mission expanded in early 2012, allowing it to conduct operations outside Mogadishu alongside TFG forces. In addition, Djibouti and Sierra Leone deployed forces, boosting AMISOM's force level to approximately 17,000 military personnel. AMISOM and TFG forces won important territorial victories throughout south and central Somalia, including recapturing the port town of Merka in Shabeelaha Hoose and the towns of Miido, El-Maan, and Sooyac in Jubbada Hoose. On September 28, coalition troops advanced toward Kismayo, sweeping in and easily ousting al Shabaab from its last urban stronghold. Public support improved for the Somali government and AMISOM, according to one opinion poll.[45] In Mogadishu, 77 percent

---

[42] "Harakat al Shabaab al-Mujahideen," *Jane's World Insurgency and Terrorism,* February 9, 2015.

[43] See, for example, Sheikh Ali Muhammed Rage, public statement, Shabelle Media Network, October 17, 2011; Rage, public statement, News24, November 16, 2011.

[44] Ahmed Abdi Godane, video statement, February 9, 2012.

[45] Since polling in Somalia is notoriously difficult, we are primarily interested in trends rather than specific numbers.

of respondents in 2012 described the TFG and AMISOM as "very effective" in stabilizing the country and encouraging reconciliation, compared with 61 and 65 percent from the previous polls in 2010 and 2011, respectively.[46]

As highlighted in Figure 2.3, by December 2012, the area where al Shabaab had freedom of movement shrank following a series of battlefield losses. In addition, public opinion polls indicated that Somalis—particularly in Mogadishu—believed their security had improved, with a decline in terrorism and insurgency-related violence. A survey in July 2012, for instance, found that an overwhelming 93 percent of respondents reported an improvement in the security situation in the past 12 months, with 4.5 percent saying it had remained the same and only 1 percent reporting a deterioration in security.[47]

In a further sign of weakness, internal fissures increased in 2012, when the American al Shabaab operative Omar Hammami launched a video attack on part of al Shabaab's leadership, which he later directed more forcefully at Godane. Hammami also criticized al Shabaab's military strategy, the marginalization of foreign fighters in the organization, sharia implementation, and al Shabaab's general mistreatment of other Muslims.[48] In response, al Shabaab tried to kill Hammami on multiple occasions, eventually succeeding.[49] Several al Shabaab leaders also announced a *fatwa* (religious ruling), removing the requirement that al Shabaab fighters be loyal to the amir if he was violating the Qur'an, which they alleged Godane was guilty of by targeting dissenters within al Shabaab.[50] These leaders included Ibrahim al-Afghani and Hassan Dahir Aweys.

---

[46] The poll was conducted by ORB International. See David Ochami and Peter Opiyo, "More Somalis Support Foreign Efforts, Says Poll," *The Standard*, March 26, 2012.

[47] Saferworld, *Mogadishu Rising? Conflict and Governance Dynamics in the Somali Capital*, London, August 2012.

[48] Omar Hammami, "Urgent Message to Whoever It Might Reach," 2012.

[49] Nicholas Kulish, "American Jihadist Is Believed to Have Been Killed by His Former Allies in Somalia," *New York Times*, September 12, 2013.

[50] SITE Intelligence Group, "Officials in Shabaab Faction Give Fatwa Against Targeting Hammami," January 15, 2014.

Figure 2.3
Al Shabaab Freedom of Movement, Late 2012

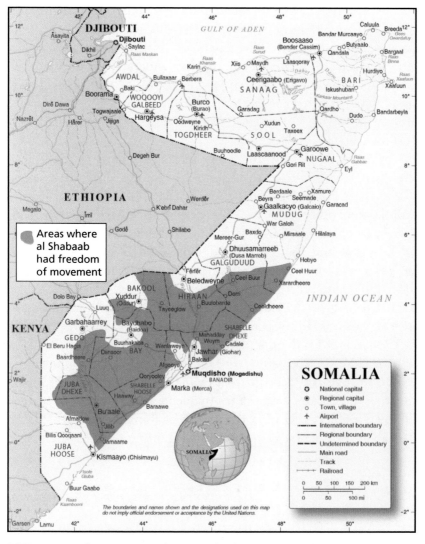

NOTE: Data are from AMISOM; the START database; Jane's World Insurgency and Terrorism database; Hansen, 2013; AFRICOM; and author estimates.

RAND RR1539-2.3

More troubling for al Shabaab, Ibrahim al-Afghani sent a letter to al Qa'ida leader Ayman al-Zawahiri objecting to Godane's leadership and requesting the appointment of a new amir. In summer 2013, these tensions erupted in unprecedented interfactional violence between forces loyal to Godane and those loyal to Mukhtar Robow, Aweys, and Shongole. An estimated 200 fighters were purged from al Shabaab's secretive Amniyat intelligence network, a support base for Godane.[51] Al Shabaab killed al-Afghani on June 20, 2013.[52] A propaganda battle also erupted, in which Robow accused Godane of failing to protect Muslims, serving as "an American spy," and neglecting to respect other Muslims.[53]

In 2013, AMISOM and TFG forces continued to make territorial gains and increased their control in former al Shabaab strongholds such as Hiran, Shabellaha Hoose, Bay-Bakool, Baidoa, Hudur, Awdinle, and Jubbada Dhexe. But despite its loss of territory, some al Shabaab operatives found sanctuary in Kenya, Uganda, Tanzania, and Ethiopia, and the semiautonomous states of northern Somalia. The loss of territory exacerbated other al Shabaab problems, including reduced financing, recruiting, and popular support.[54] Still, al Shabaab conducted high-profile assassinations and suicide attacks in Somalia, targeting the Somali president in September 2013, the chief of security in March 2013, the presidential compound in February 2014, the Supreme Court in April 2013, the UN Development Programme headquarters in June 2013, the international airport in February 2014, and numerous hotels and restaurants frequented by Somali government and foreign officials. During the month of Ramadan in July 2014, al Shabaab's assassination campaign in Mogadishu claimed the lives of

---

[51] Menkhaus, 2014.

[52] Hansen, 2014, pp. 9–12.

[53] Zubair al-Muhajir, "Yes There Is a Problem—Open Letter from Sheikh Zubayr al-Muhajir to Sheikh Abu al-Zubair," April 18, 2013; Ibrahim al-Afghani, "Urgent and Open Letter to Our Amiir Shaykh Ayman al-Zawahiri," April 2013; Mukhtar Robow, "The Martyrdom Night in Barawe [and What Happened] Before and After It," audio recording, September 19, 2013.

[54] Menkhaus, 2014.

more than 100 security officials, politicians, and civil servants.[55] In April 2015, al Shabaab orchestrated another deadly attack, this time at Garissa University in the heavily Somali-populated northeastern province of Kenya. In October 2015, al Shabaab called for expanded attacks against a range of targets, from the Russian government to Jews across the globe.[56]

But as Figure 2.4 highlights, by late 2016, al Shabaab's freedom of movement shrank to a small area around the Lower Jubba River Valley following a series of AMISOM operations described in Chapter Three, although al Shabaab's freedom of movement increased slightly in 2016 following operations in such areas as Merka.

After losing control of many of its seaport revenues and suffering declining diaspora support, al Shabaab attempted to adapt by extracting coercive "taxes" from local businesses, humanitarian organizations, and nongovernmental organizations (NGOs).[57] But the loss of Kismayo was particularly devastating, contributing to a loss of tens of millions of dollars annually for al Shabaab.[58] More broadly, al Shabaab's coastal losses impacted the group's revenue base, which benefited from port operations and taxes on goods.[59] In such areas as Baardheere and Diinsoor, which the group lost in July 2015, al Shabaab had derived most of its funding from taxation of trade and other forms of business occurring in, or passing through, its area of control. The group also taxed farmers in its territory.[60] Counterpiracy efforts along the Somalia

---

[55] See Appendix for a detailed list of mass-casualty events and high-profile assassinations in the history of al Shabaab.

[56] Al Shabaab, "Support Al-Aqsa Mosque," statement posted on the deep web jihadi forums Shumukh al-Islam and al-Fida', October 10, 2015.

[57] Menkhaus, 2014.

[58] According to some estimates, the port of Kismayo was al Shabaab's largest source of internal revenue, in particular from charcoal exports and sugar cane imports. See Armin Rosen, "How Africa's Most Threatening Terrorist Group Lost Control of Somalia," *Atlantic*, September 21, 2012.

[59] Roble, 2015, p. 2.

[60] Jane's World Insurgency and Terrorism, "Harakat al Shabaab al-Mujahideen," February 9, 2015.

Figure 2.4
Al Shabaab Freedom of Movement, Late 2016

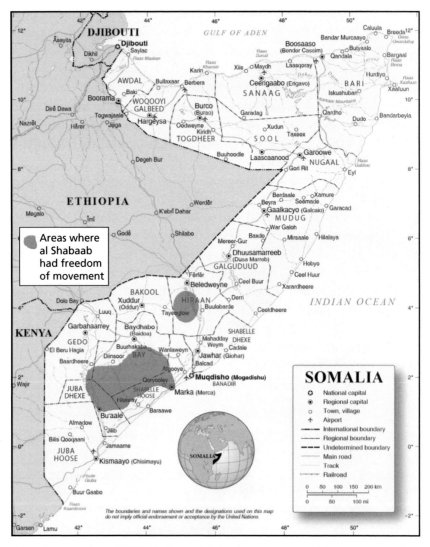

NOTE: Data are from AMISOM; the START database; Jane's World Insurgency and Terrorism database; and author estimates.

RAND *RR1539-2.4*

coast also undermined al Shabaab's financing, as did efforts in such neighboring states as Kenya to target al Shabaab's sources of revenue, recruitment, and propaganda. Still, despite al Shabaab's loss of key coastal cities, al Shabaab still collected some finances from illicit trafficking out of Indian Ocean ports, including Baraawe.

Despite progress in pushing al Shabaab out of areas it once controlled, the organization is still dangerous and lethal. It conducted an increasingly violent terrorist campaign, shifting from an insurgent group that controlled territory to a terrorist group that commits indiscriminate attacks on civilians and combatants alike. These attacks—including al Shabaab's targeting of civilians, AMISOM forces, and Somali government officials—underscores that the campaign against it is far from over. Al Shabaab leaders have indicated their desire to increase control of territory, which would allow them to collect more taxes, profiting from port activity; recruit more supporters; and oversee an Islamic emirate. Still, the group retains an ability to conduct attacks and disrupt normal life in Somalia and neighboring countries such as Kenya.

The number of al Shabaab attacks rose each year from 2007 to 2014 but declined somewhat in 2015. Figure 2.5 highlights data from the START database and ACLED. The Appendix includes a more robust discussion of possible reasons for the differences between the two databases. The decline in al Shabaab attacks in 2015 may have been a result of sustained AMISOM efforts during Operation Jubba Corridor, when al Shabaab lost control of such cities as Baardheere and Diinsoor. These operations put al Shabaab on the defensive. Still, both databases indicate that al Shabaab violence in 2015 was higher than every other year since 2007, except for 2014, highlighting the group's sustained ability to conduct attacks. The trend in fatalities is similar for both databases, with fatality numbers peaking in 2014 and then declining somewhat in the START database and leveling off in the ACLED database. Again, these trends suggest that al Shabaab remains a lethal organization capable of conducting attacks and killing combatants and noncombatants.

Figure 2.5
Al Shabaab Attacks, 2007–2015

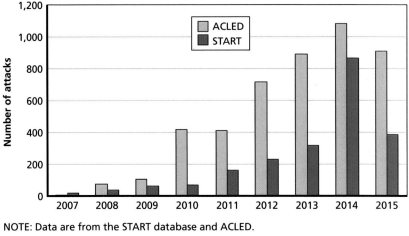

NOTE: Data are from the START database and ACLED.

RAND *RR1539-2.5*

The high number of attacks may have been caused by several factors.[61] First, al Shabaab leaders were likely trying to coerce the withdrawal of foreign forces, particularly AMISOM forces, by punishing their civilians. Al Shabaab focused in particular on civilian targets in Kenya. Second, al Shabaab may have increased terrorist attacks in order to bait governments such as Somalia and Kenya into overreacting. In past insurgencies, the goal of a baiting strategy is that governments and their security forces are so appalled at the killing of civilians that their military response is excessive. In Northern Ireland, the Irish Republican Army (IRA) used terrorism in the 1970s to bait British forces into overreacting, which they did during Bloody Sunday, the Falls Road Curfew, and internment operations. British practices sparked an

---

[61] The data may also underrepresent the actual number of attacks due to several factors, such as how terrorist attacks were coded, public claims by perpetrators, and whether journalists wrote about the attacks. This is particularly true in the earlier years of al Shabaab's existence, before it had developed sophisticated media and Internet operations. Nonetheless, we have tried to mitigate these concerns by carefully reviewing the information behind these numbers and adding additional cases where appropriate. For a more detailed discussion of data collection sources and notes, see the Appendix of this report.

upsurge in violence and a wave of support for the IRA. Third, al Shabaab may have increased attacks simply to enact revenge. Fourth, the loss of territory may have allowed al Shabaab to use resources for terrorist attacks that the group's leaders otherwise would have used for establishing law and order in territory that they controlled.

Based on these possible motivations, al Shabaab's attacks increasingly targeted Kenya, AMISOM forces, and Somali government officials as well as soft targets. In September 2013, al Shabaab operatives grabbed international headlines by conducting a deadly attack at the upscale Westgate Mall in Nairobi, Kenya, killing at least 59 people and wounding nearly 200 others. The attack was well planned and involved careful intelligence collection, surveillance, and reconnaissance of the mall. In November 2013, al Shabaab released a special edition of its magazine, *Gaidi Mtaani*, devoted to the mall attack. The magazine justified the attack as retaliation for Kenya's alleged "blatant aggression against Islam and Muslims," as well as Kenya's purported "blind and aimless bombardment of civilians by Kenyan jets and ships."[62] Al Shabaab continued to conduct a broad campaign in 2016 by attempting to overrun AMISOM bases, attacking Somali National Army bases, and conducting a range of assassinations and bombings in Mogadishu and other cities.

These terrorist attacks may have reinforced al Shabaab's terrorist credentials but generally undermined the group's popular support in Somalia, a concern raised by al Shabaab leadership. As al Shabaab leader Fuad Mohamed Khalaf acknowledged,

"The reason the holy warriors have failed to emerge victorious against the infidels is largely due to the bad relationship between the public and al Shabaab . . . If we are stronger than the public, we should remember that Allah is also stronger than us . . . We need to fairly treat people if we are to succeed."[63]

---

[62] "From the Editor," *Gaidi Mtaani*, Dhul Hijra 1434, toleo 4, p. 1.

[63] "Losing Streak—Public Support Fades for al-Shabab," *AMISOM*, September 2011.

According to public opinion polls conducted in Kenya, al Shabaab's Garissa attack contributed to a rise in anti–al Shabaab perceptions among Kenyans, as well as a desire for Kenyan forces to remain in Somalia. But it also contributed to growing concerns in Kenya that the country was headed in the wrong direction and that al Shabaab posed a serious and rising terrorist threat in Kenya.[64]

Conclusion

As this chapter highlights, al Shabaab's strength varied over five phases of its existence. Its territorial control peaked between 2009 and 2010 in the aftermath of the Ethiopian invasion, and then declined over the next several years. By 2016, al Shabaab had lost substantial territory and had suffered from a series of leadership and organizational disputes. It also suffered a significant decline in revenue following its military defeats, since the group had derived much of its funding by taxing individuals, businesses, and groups in areas it controlled. Al Shabaab's popular support also dwindled in Somalia and neighboring countries, including Kenya. Despite these losses, however, al Shabaab increased the number of terrorist attacks, suggesting that it shifted from an insurgent group that controlled territory and governed its inhabitants to a terrorist organization that controlled little territory but increasingly relied on terrorist tactics.

---

[64] Mohammed Yusuf, "Poll: Eight in 10 Kenyans See Al-Shabab as 'Major Threat,'" *Voice of America*, April 17, 2015.

CHAPTER THREE
The Weakening of al Shabaab

As the previous chapter outlined, al Shabaab suffered a steady string of battlefield setbacks beginning in 2011. By 2016, al Shabaab had lost much of the territory it once controlled, though it still remained capable of conducting regular grisly terrorist attacks in Somalia and the region. What factors contributed to the weakening of al Shabaab? This chapter finds that the "tailored engagement" strategy eventually adopted—which involved a combination of AMISOM-led (often supported by the United States) ground operations, U.S. precision strikes, and U.S. and other allied capacity-building efforts—severely degraded al Shabaab. This strategy weakened al Shabaab by using only a small number of U.S. forces, which did not expose American soldiers to the risk of heavy casualties or expand the U.S. military footprint to levels that might spur nationalist or religious blowback.

The rest of this chapter is divided into two main sections. The first examines strategic options available to the United States and other Western allies to counter al Shabaab, all of which have been tried in Somalia over the past several decades. The second outlines the tailored engagement strategy that contributed to the weakening of al Shabaab.

Strategic Options

As used here, a strategy includes a government's resources and methods to degrade or defeat adversaries, including terrorist or insurgent groups.[1] A strategy requires officials to foresee the nature of the war. Do the resources and methods—the proposed strategy—promise success at a reasonable cost? The British soldier and military theorist B. H. Liddell Hart referred to strategy as "the art of distributing and applying military means to fulfill the ends of policy."[2] Strategy includes not just military means, but political, economic, and other instruments as well. Strategy in this sense is different from a *grand strategy*, which is the broader process (usually by a state) of determining vital security interests, identifying the threats to those interests, and deciding how best to employ political, military, and economic resources to protect those interests.[3] Strategy also should be distinguished from *tactics*, which include the techniques for using weapons or military units in combination to engage and defeat an adversary.

There are several strategic options available to the United States and other Western countries against al Shabaab: indirect engagement, robust intervention, and tailored engagement. These strategies are intended to be generalizations, and there are numerous variations within each of them.

Indirect engagement: The first option involves relying only on *other* forces—not U.S. forces—to conduct targeted strikes or train local security forces.[4] We call this strategy *indirect engagement*. It can sometimes be a preferable option because the United States minimizes the use of its own forces, money, and credibility in pursuing its objectives. This strategy seeks to minimize foreign entanglements and limit costs and risks. For counterterrorism and counterinsurgency, it is less

---

[1] On strategy, see, for example, Lawrence Freedman, *Strategy: A History*, New York: Oxford University Press, 2013, pp. ix–xvi. Also see John J. Mearsheimer, *Conventional Deterrence*, Ithaca, N.Y.: Cornell University Press, 1983, pp. 2, 28–29.

[2] B. H. Liddell Hart, *Strategy: The Indirect Approach*, London: Faber, 1967, p. 335.

[3] On grand strategy see Barry R. Posen, *The Sources of Military Doctrine: France, Britain, and Germany Between the World Wars*, Ithaca, N.Y.: Cornell University Press, 1984, p. 13; Hart, 1967, pp. 335–336.

[4] Some have called this strategy "buck-passing." See, for example, Mancur Olson, Jr., *The Logic of Collective Action: Public Goods and the Theory of Groups*, Cambridge, Mass.: Harvard University Press, 1965; Barry Posen, 1984; John J. Mearsheimer, *The Tragedy of Great Power Politics*, New York: W. W. Norton, 2001.

likely than other strategies to inflame local populations that may bristle at direct U.S. military involvement, including in Muslim countries. In Somalia, indirect engagement would involve deferring all military action against al Shabaab to Somali government forces, nonstate actors, other Western governments, or regional powers, such as Kenya and Ethiopia. The United States adopted this strategy in the mid-2000s.

But indirect engagement has several downsides. First, it is too risky in cases where terrorist groups are actively plotting attacks against the United States or U.S. structures (such as embassies) abroad. Without a U.S. presence, indirect engagement significantly reduces America's ability to influence the situation because allies may not always share U.S. interests or capabilities. This may be acceptable in cases where terrorist groups are not plotting attacks against the U.S. homeland or its interests overseas. But it is precarious in situations where there is an imminent threat. Second, indirect engagement does not necessarily undermine the extremist narrative of terrorist and insurgent groups such as al Shabaab. After al Shabaab's public merger with al Qa'ida in 2012, which resulted in closer ties between the two organizations, the group became an increasingly serious potential threat to U.S. interests in East Africa. Of particular concern was al Shabaab's relationship with al Qa'ida in the Arabian Peninsula, which plotted a series of attacks against the U.S. homeland from its base in Yemen.

Despite the absence of U.S. direct engagement in the late 2000s, al Shabaab leaders saw the United States as an enemy because of the unwillingness of the United States to accept the preeminence of Islamic law. In addition, Ethiopia's 2006 unilateral military intervention in Somalia generated a wave of radical nationalist and religious sentiment among Somalis at home and abroad.[5] In response, al Shabaab held an effective propaganda campaign against Ethiopia using its media wing, the Al-Kataib Foundation for Media Productions. It also used the Internet and several radio stations—such as Quran Karim Radio FM,

---

5   Oscar Gakuo Mwangi, "State Collapse, Al Shabaab, Islamism, and Legitimacy in Somalia," *Politics, Religion and Ideology*, Vol. 13, No. 4, December 2012, pp. 513–527; John C. Amble and Alexander Meleagrou-Hitchens, "Jihadist Radicalization in East Africa: Two Case Studies," *Studies in Conflict and Terrorism*, Vol. 37, 2014, pp. 523–540.

Somali Wayen Radio FM, HornAfrik Radio, and Radio Al-Andalus—
to disseminate its jihadist rhetoric and portray the movement as a pro-
vider of basic economic and political goods and services. Without U.S.
or broader AMISOM direct engagement, al Shabaab became the de
facto government in key parts of Somalia. It provided such services as
education, justice, security, medical care, food, and local-level administration and public works. Al Shabaab operatives often conducted a
koormeer, or visit, where its fighters visited towns and villages to gain
legitimacy. Al Shabaab religious leaders also addressed the population in public and discussed the need for changes, explaining what the
movement could do for the Somali people. By 2010, al Shabaab was
the strongest, best-organized, best-financed, and best-armed military
group that controlled the largest stretch of territory in southern Somalia, a major blow to U.S. indirect engagement.[6]

Robust intervention: The second strategy involves direct and relatively large-scale U.S. military involvement to fight adversaries, what
we call robust intervention. Unlike indirect engagement, it can include
a range of U.S. military, political, and other steps to degrade or defeat
terrorist and insurgent groups. The size, force posture, and force pack-
ages can vary considerably. Since World War II, for example, U.S. peak
military presence has varied from 19.3 forces per 1,000 inhabitants
in Kosovo (1999) and 17.5 forces per thousand inhabitants in Bosnia
(1995), to much-lower ratios, such as 2.9 forces per 1,000 inhabitants in Haiti (1994). In Somalia, the peak U.S. military presence in
the 1990s was 5.7 troops per 1,000 inhabitants (1992).[7] U.S. forces in
Somalia participated in the UNITAF, which lasted from December
1992 to May 1993, and UNOSOM II, which lasted from March 1993
to March 1995. UNITAF's mission was to provide security for the
relief effort. The initial arrival in December 1992 of U.S. troops as part
of UNITAF led to a substantial diminution of conflict between war-

---

[6] Mwangi, 2012, pp. 513–527.

[7] James Dobbins, Seth G. Jones, Keith Crane, Christopher S. Chivvis, Andrew Radin, F.
Stephen Larrabee, Nora Bensahel, Brooke Stearns Lawson, and Benjamin W. Goldsmith,
Europe's Role in Nation-Building: From the Balkans to the Congo, Santa Monica, Calif.:
RAND Corporation, MG-722-RC, 2008, p. 243.

lords and a period of relative quiescence. UNITAF included 28,000 U.S. troops who were authorized to use decisive force if necessary.[8]

The UN began the transition from UNITAF to UNOSOM II in March 1993, and authority was formally transferred on May 4, 1993. UNOSOM II held a much broader mandate than UNITAF and was authorized to use force against armed combatants beyond cases of self-defense. Despite this expanded mandate, the authorized strength of UNOSOM II was 28,000, significantly smaller than UNITAF. At its height, UNOSOM II and the U.S. quick reaction force comprised 17,500 troops, short of UNOSOM II's authorized strength and even shorter of its effective combat power.[9] The security situation grew increasingly unstable as Somali warlords became hostile to the UN troops. On June 5, 1993, Somali fighters, allegedly from the warlord Mohamed Farah Aideed's militia, killed 25 Pakistani peacekeepers. The UN Secretary General was outraged at these killings, which occurred when the soldiers were unloading food at a feeding station.[10] The United States deployed Task Force Ranger in late August 1993, and U.S. forces conducted a series of raids in September. As highlighted in the Box 3.1, 18 U.S. soldiers were killed on October 3 and 4 during an operation against Aideed's forces.[11]

While there are some benefits to a robust intervention strategy, it, too, has several downsides in Somalia. First, substantial U.S. engagement could embolden the narrative of al Shabaab and other Salafi-jihadist groups, who would invariably attempt to portray the conflict as one between Islam and infidel countries. This would increase the likelihood of blowback. Indeed, the U.S. deployment of conventional

---

[8] Nora Bensahel, "Humanitarian Relief and Nation Building in Somalia," in Robert J. Art and Patrick M. Cronin, eds., *The United States and Coercive Diplomacy*, Washington, D.C.: United States Institute of Peace Press, 2003, pp. 20–56.

[9] David Bentley and Robert Oakley, "Peace Operations: A Comparison of Somalia and Haiti," National Defense University, *Strategic Forum*, No. 30, May 1995.

[10] UN, 1996, pp. 299–300.

[11] The formal mandate changed in 1993. The mission also morphed from one that was focused to a great degree on meeting humanitarian needs to one more directly involved in attempting to resolve Somalia's political problems. The United States became increasingly involved in clan politics, favoring—or being perceived as favoring—some clans over others.

Box 3.1: Black Hawk Down

On October 3, 1993, Task Force Ranger received intelligence about a meeting of senior officials from Mohamed Farah Aideed's clan. The United States launched an operation to seize these officials and possibly Aideed. During the operation, Somali militia shot down two Black Hawk helicopters, leading U.S. forces to delay their withdrawal as they worked to rescue the downed crew. The complicated U.S. and UN command structure created significant delays in coordinating the rescue effort. As a result, U.S. forces spent the night fighting off Somali militia before being extracted by U.S. and UN forces the next morning. Eighteen U.S. soldiers were killed in the firefight, and one was captured alive. This action led the administration of President Bill Clinton to set a deadline for the withdrawal of U.S. forces from Somalia by March 31, 1994.

---

forces to fight terrorists overseas has often been counterproductive. While some conventional forces in Iraq and Afghanistan occasionally achieved their military objectives and degraded al Qa'ida and other groups' capabilities, they also had the unintended consequence of contributing to creating a new generation of terrorists. In Iraq, for instance, the large U.S. presence and the way the United States occupied the country, including the imprisonment of tens of thousands of Sunnis, contributed to radicalization. In general, large numbers of U.S. forces tend to facilitate terrorist and insurgent recruitment and propaganda efforts. Many of the terrorists involved in serious homeland plots after September 11, 2001—from Nidal Hasan's 2009 mass shooting at Fort Hood to Najibullah Zazi's 2009 terrorist plot in New York City—were motivated, in part, by the deployment of large numbers of U.S. combat troops in Muslim countries and by a conviction, however misplaced, that Muslims were helpless victims.[12] Second, building public support for robust engagement, particularly in Somalia, is difficult. Third,

---

[12] Seth G. Jones, *Hunting in the Shadows: The Pursuit of Al Qa'ida Since 9/11*, New York: W. W. Norton, 2012.

there are greater financial costs with a robust intervention strategy than with the other strategies examined here, and they put American soldiers and other government officials at greater risk.

Tailored engagement: The third strategy involves a light military footprint—particularly the use of special operations forces—in which foreign forces conduct limited strikes and train, advise, assist, and accompany local forces to degrade or defeat insurgent and terrorist groups.[13] Tailored engagement is distinct from indirect engagement in that U.S. forces deploy to the targeted country and directly fight insurgent or terrorist groups. It is different from robust intervention, since it involves small numbers of forces, typically special operations forces, and aims to work by, with, and through local partners. These local partners can include the host nation, other countries, or nonstate actors, such as tribal or clan forces. In some cases, direct U.S. engagement may be limited to such options as covert action by intelligence operatives or special operations forces acting under Title 50 of the United States Code, which allows military forces to conduct intelligence activities such as covert action.[14] Examples of tailored engagement include

- precision air strikes from drones, fixed-wing aircraft, or helicopters to capture or kill terrorists or insurgents
- raids to capture or kill terrorists or insurgents, free hostages, seize their supplies for intelligence collection and exploitation, or target their finances

---

[13] On a similar approach see, for example, Linda Robinson, *The Future of U.S. Special Operations Forces*, New York: Council on Foreign Relations, 2013; Linda Robinson, "The Future of Special Operations: Beyond Kill and Capture," *Foreign Affairs*, Vol. 91, No. 6, November/December 2012.

[14] As outlined in the National Security Act of 1947, covert action refers to "an activity or activities of the United States Government to influence political, economic, or military conditions abroad, where it is intended that the role of the United States Government will not be apparent or acknowledged publicly." See United States Code, Title 50, Section 3001, National Security Act of 1947, sec. 503(e), enacted December 18, 2015. In addition, Title 50 of the U.S. Code allows the U.S. military to conduct covert action under a CIA-run operation. See United States Code, Title 50, Section 413, War and National Defense, amended April 21, 2005.

- operational planning and advice to foreign headquarters, division, brigade, battalion, and perhaps company levels
- civil affairs operations, such as assessments; community outreach; water, education, and health projects; and construction of roads, bridges, and airstrips
- information and psychological operations
- intelligence support operations, including the creation and running of fusion centers
- logistics support
- medical evacuation, emergency medical care, quick reaction, and combat search and rescue via air and maritime mobility platforms
- training of army and other ground units in a wide variety of operational and tactical skills, from sniper tactics to countering improvised explosive devices
- training of air crews in night-vision capability, forward air control, close air support, and casualty and medical evacuation
- training of maritime forces in interdiction and other operations
- training of police forces
- training, equipping, institutional support and advisory services
- accompany forces into—or in proximity to—combat zones.[15]

As with all strategies, there are risks with tailored engagement. First, the success of tailored engagement depends on the competence and will of local partners, which can be limited or even nonexistent. In Yemen, for example, the United States lost its partner led by Yemeni President Abed Rabbo Mansour Hadi when Houthi militants overthrew the government in 2015. Second, direct U.S. engagement, even a lower-profile presence, could embolden the narrative of terrorist and insurgent groups, who will invariably attempt to portray the conflict as one between Islam and the West. Direct U.S. participation will likely become public, despite efforts to keep it clandestine. Third, there is a potential for mission creep. In Afghanistan, for example, the United States gradually raised its military footprint from several hundred in 2001 to approximately 100,000 by 2010 and became increasingly

---

[15] We thank Linda Robinson for helping us identify key tasks.

involved in nation building. Fourth, there is some potential for blow-back. In cases where terrorist and insurgent groups are not interested in targeting the U.S. homeland or its embassies, U.S. strikes against the group could cause a change in their behavior. After the 2009 U.S. killing of Tehreek-e-Taliban Pakistan (TTP) leader Baitullah Mehsud, for example, the TTP became increasingly interested in targeting the United States. In May 2010, Faisal Shahzad attempted to detonate a car bomb in Times Square, New York City, after being trained by TTP leaders in Pakistan. Fourth, building the capacity of local governments is an extremely difficult task, including in countries such as Somalia that have low levels of governance capacity.

But the benefits of an engagement strategy outweigh the risks in most cases where terrorist groups are *already* plotting attacks against the U.S. homeland or its interests overseas (such as U.S. embassies), especially where the local government has minimal capabilities or little political will to counter groups. In these cases, a U.S. failure to become directly engaged could severely jeopardize U.S. national security if a group were to strike the U.S. homeland or a U.S. embassy. The risks of not being engaged could be serious. The death of Americans would likely have political costs if Americans concluded that U.S. policymakers did not do enough to prevent an attack. Still, the possibility that direct U.S. engagement could inflame the local population suggests that U.S. policymakers should carefully weigh the type of engagement.

The Decline of al Shabaab

Since the 2011 AMISOM offensive around Mogadishu, the United States has pursued a tailored engagement strategy in Somalia. This section highlights key elements of the strategy, which were successful in weakening al Shabaab. Beginning in 2011, the campaign involved AMISOM-led ground operations; U.S. and other Western efforts to build partner capacity, conduct limited kinetic strikes, and help coordinate AMISOM efforts; and other factors, such as al Shabaab internal flaws and missteps during the East African famine. These factors are interlinked. It is unlikely that AMISOM would have conducted a successful ground campaign without U.S. and other Western assistance. In addition, U.S. strikes would likely have failed to dislodge al Shabaab from southern Somalia without AMISOM ground operations. And U.S. and AMISOM military operations might have been vastly more difficult had al Shabaab not suffered a series of debilitating internal struggles.

One factor that contributed to the weakening of al Shabaab was the leading role of neighboring AMISOM countries in conducting a ground campaign, though some of their operations were conducted unilaterally rather than through AMISOM's command and control. Since one of al Shabaab's objectives is to seize and occupy territory—which allows the group to collect finances, recruit fighters, and govern territory through its extreme interpretation of sharia—a successful strategy needs to involve retaking territory. While there are numerous factors that contribute to the demise of terrorist and insurgent groups, denying groups territorial control is critical.[16] Some research shows that local security forces are particularly important in degrading or defeating groups.[17]

AMISOM's start was inauspicious. It was authorized by the UN Security Council in February 2007 under Chapter VII of the UN charter to help reestablish and train Somali security forces, contribute to the security conditions necessary for humanitarian assistance, and support dialogue and reconciliation among the warring parties.[18] Yet African leaders were reluctant to commit troops to Somalia's unstable environment, and AMISOM suffered chronic delays in the deployment of soldiers and the acquisition of equipment over the first several years, making it largely irrelevant on the battlefield. As Chapter Two discussed, al Shabaab had expanded its control of territory by 2010,

---

[16] On how terrorist and insurgent groups end, see Audrey Kurth Cronin, *How Terrorism Ends: Understanding the Decline and Demise of Terrorist Campaigns*, Princeton, N.J.: Princeton University Press, 2009; Ben Connable and Martin Libicki, *How Insurgencies End*, Santa Monica, Calif.: RAND Corporation, MG-965-MCIA, 2010; Seth G. Jones, *Conducting Insurgent Warfare*, New York: Oxford University Press, forthcoming.

[17] Seth G. Jones and Martin C. Libicki, *How Terrorist Groups End: Lessons for Countering Al Qa'ida*, Santa Monica, Calif.: RAND Corporation, MG-741-1-RC, 2008.

[18] United Nations Security Council, "Resolution 1744," S/RES/1744, February 21, 2007.

seizing the majority of south-central Somalia and limiting the TFG and AMISOM forces to a few neighborhood blocks in Mogadishu.[19]

The situation began to change in 2011. Kenya and Ethiopia, which border Somalia, launched military operations to blunt al Shabaab activity that was undermining their security. AMISOM forces, led by Uganda and Burundi, launched offensive operations beginning in February, clearing most of Mogadishu over the next several months. In addition, Kenyan and Somalian military forces initiated Operation Linda Nchi in October 2011 in southern Somalia. This effort, which began during the rainy season, was slowed by bad weather. Supported by Kenyan air, ground, and naval assets, Kenyan forces and clan militias seized such cities as Afmadow, approximately 70 miles northwest of Kismayo, laying the groundwork for subsequent efforts to retake Kismayo. Ethiopian forces then reentered Somalia to attack al Shabaab positions in the west under AMISOM auspices.[20] In February 2012, the UN Security Council adopted resolution 2036, asking AMISOM to extend its presence beyond Mogadishu and authorizing the use of "all necessary measures . . . to reduce the threat posed by al Shabaab."[21]

Al Shabaab suffered another blow in September 2012, when AMISOM and Somali National Army forces launched Operation Sledge Hammer, pushing al Shabaab out of the southern port city of Kismayo.[22] As in several previous AMISOM operations, al Shabaab fighters were reticent to engage in conventional battles with AMISOM forces and instead withdrew their forces, probably assuming they would be able to return once AMISOM forces withdrew from the city. But AMISOM countries did not withdraw.

In 2014, AMISOM and Somali National Army forces conducted two major offensive operations, which significantly reduced

---

[19] Noel Anderson, "Peacekeepers Fighting a Counterinsurgency Campaign: A Net Assessment of the African Union Mission in Somalia," *Studies in Conflict and Terrorism*, Vol. 37, No. 11, 2014, pp. 936–958.

[20] Anderson, 2014, pp. 936–958.

[21] United Nations Security Council, "Resolution 2036," S/RES/2036, February 22, 2012.

[22] Sudarsan Raghavan, "Kenyan Military Says It Has Driven Al-Shabab Militia from Its Last Stronghold in Somalia," *Washington Post*, September 28, 2012.

the territory controlled by al Shabaab. These operations benefited from the formal introduction of more than 4,000 Ethiopian troops into AMISOM in January 2014, bolstering the number of African Union troops to 22,126.[23] Within a month of the arrival of Ethiopian reinforcements, the Somali National Army and AMISOM launched a major offensive, Operation Eagle. Ethiopian and Somali troops captured several strategic towns in the regions of Bay, Bakool, and Gedo in southwestern Somalia near the Ethiopian border. Forces from Uganda, Burundi, Djibouti, and Ethiopia also retook territory from al Shabaab in the Lower and Middle Shabelle regions during this period, as well as Hiiraan and Galgadud.[24] Following the end of Ramadan in August 2014, AMISOM launched its second major offensive of the year, Operation Indian Ocean, to retake several strategic towns along the coast. AMISOM forces, led by Burundi and Uganda, cleared several key towns, such as Baraawe, Bulo Marer, and Cadale, as highlighted in Figure 3.1.[25]

Al Shabaab's loss of Baraawe in October 2014 was particularly damaging, since the port city was a safe haven for its fighters and an important source of revenue because it served as the main hub for the group's multimillion-dollar charcoal trade. Al Shabaab also lost Tiyeeglow district, an important logistical hub located approximately 300 miles northwest of Mogadishu, in the Bakool region.[26] As a result, the group did not control a district in the four regions of Bakool, Hiiraan, and Lower and Middle Shabelle in southern Somalia. Still, al Shabaab was not defeated. In Gedo region, it still controlled Baardheere, the largest and most populated district. It also controlled Diinsoor and Ufurow in Bay region; Jamaame and Kamsuma in Lower Juba; Bu'aale, Sakow, and Jilib in Middle Juba; Eldher in Galgadud; and Harardhere

---

[23] "Ethiopian Troops Formally Join AMISOM Peacekeepers in Somalia," *AMISOM News*, January 2014.

[24] Muhyadin Ahmed Roble, "Al-Shabaab: On the Back Foot But Still Dangerous," *Militant Leadership Monitor*, Vol. 13, No. 2, April 2015, p. 2.

[25] AMISOM, "Joint Security Update on Operation Indian Ocean by Somali Government and AMISOM," October 29, 2014.

[26] Roble, 2015, p. 2.

Figure 3.1
Operation Indian Ocean, August–October 2014

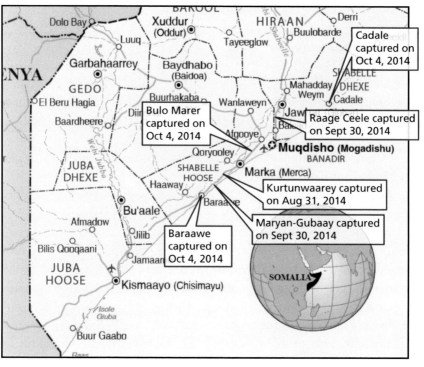

RAND RR1539-3.1

in Mudug. Al Shabaab conducted a series of attacks, including those led by the group's intelligence unit, Amniyat, and its military wing, Jabhad.[27]

In July 2014, AMISOM countries conducted Operation Jubba Corridor to retake such areas as Diinsoor and Baardheere, as illustrated in Figure 3.2. Baardheere had been under the control of al Shabaab for more than seven years. Ethiopian, Kenyan, and Somali forces

---

[27] Sunguta West, "Al Shabaab to Face Different Direction after Appointment of New Leader," *Militant Leadership Monitor*, April 2015, p. 7; Sunguta West, "Al Shabaab to Face Different Direction after Appointment of New Leader," *Militant Leadership Monitor*, April 2015, p. 7.

successfully retook Baardheere on July 22, and Ethiopian and Somali forces retook Diinsoor on July 24. U.S. forces provided direct assistance in the vicinity of both Baardheere and Diinsoor, which was particularly useful, since al Shabaab had prepared to engage AMISOM forces in conventional operations using relatively large formations of several hundred fighters. A range of strikes in July, however, killed several dozen al Shabaab fighters, causing them to withdraw from Baardheere and Diinsoor. By early 2016, AMISOM forces had cleared much of southern Somalia. Al Shabaab's freedom of movement had shrunk to a small area, mostly along the Jubba River Valley in such towns as Saacow, Jilib, Bulaale, and Jamaane. And thousands of Somalis continued to return to Somalia from neighboring countries and by airplane into Mogadishu International Airport.[28]

As discussed in Chapter Four, however, numerous challenges remain in Somalia. The Somali government and Somali National Army forces are weak and poorly trained, and AMISOM countries frequently turned to clan militias to help fill the political and security vacuums following al Shabaab's withdrawal. In addition, many AMISOM countries regularly divert their attention and resources to dealing with their own security priorities, such as fighting in South Sudan or combatting the Lord's Resistance Army. AMISOM itself continues to suffer from coordination problems among its troop-contributing countries and substantial logistics, manpower, and equipment shortfalls.

U.S. and Other Western Support

U.S. and broader Western assistance to AMISOM countries, Somali National Army forces, and nonstate actors such as clan militias also contributed to the weakening of al Shabaab. This section focuses on U.S. assistance, although a number of European countries and organizations—such as the United Kingdom, France, and the European Union—also provided aid and training. The European Union Train-

---

[28] United Nations High Commissioner for Refugees, "Return to Somalia: No Longer a Refugee," August 7, 2015; Laila Ali, "Somalia: on the Run Again—Somali Refugees Return Home from Yemen," August 28, 2015; Abdulaziz Billow, "Somali Refugees Sail Home from Yemen," Voice of America, August 19, 2015. Ironically, some of the refugees who returned to Somalia were fleeing from other conflicts, including Yemen.

Figure 3.2
Operation Jubba Corridor, July 2015

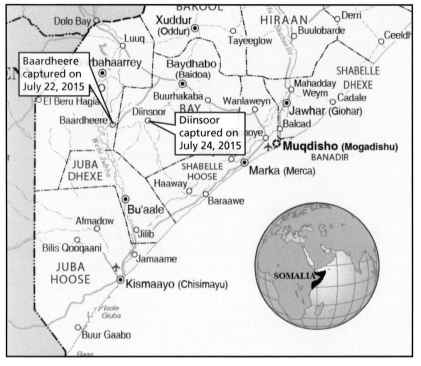

RAND RR1539-3.2

ing Mission, for example, provided training and assistance to Somali government forces and security institutions.[29] U.S. assistance involved three broad components: training, advising, assisting, and occasionally accompanying AMISOM and Somali forces; conducting targeted strikes; and helping coordinate activities with AMISOM leaders.

First, the United States provided training, advice, and assistance to AMISOM and Somali forces. U.S. military forces, for instance, helped train the Kenyan 40th Ranger Strike Forces, Kenyan Special

---

[29] See, for example, European Union External Action, "Factsheet on EUTM Somalia," October 2014; Council of the European Union, "Somalia: EU Extends Training Mission," March 16, 2015.

Boat Unit, and Ugandan People's Defense Force Special Forces Group. Training covered information operations, civil affairs, field medical skills, medical evacuation skills, maintenance, command and control, personnel management, and logistics.[30] Some U.S. conventional forces also provided training to AMISOM countries in such areas as logistics, communications, and medical support. The U.S. Department of Defense (DoD) funded these efforts under Sections 1206, 1207, and other authorities of the National Defense Authorization Act.[31] In addition, the Africa Contingency Operations Training and Assistance program, housed within the State Department's Bureau of African Affairs, funded efforts to enhance the capacity of AMISOM forces. The State Department also used Bancroft Global Development to train and advise AMISOM forces and the Somali National Army in combat operations and support functions.[32] Finally, the United States, other Western governments, and AMISOM countries provided limited assistance to some Somalia clan militias.

It is challenging to assess the impact of U.S. support on the performance of AMISOM and Somali forces, since there are numerous factors—not just outside aid—that influenced these outcomes. Nevertheless, there is some evidence that U.S. assistance contributed to improved performance. Kenyan special operations forces, for example, conducted several complex, joint amphibious assaults on the Somali port of Kismayo during Operation Indian Ocean, facilitated in part by U.S. training. Kenyan forces also were able to retake Baardheere in July 2015 during Operation Jubba Corridor thanks to U.S. assistance.[33]

Second, the United States was involved in several types of direct action and information collection against al Shabaab. One was joint

---

[30] Author discussions with Kenyan and Ugandan officials, July 2015.

[31] Lauren Ploch Blanchard, *The September 2013 Terrorist Attack in Kenya: In Brief*, Washington, D.C.: Congressional Research Service, November 14, 2013; Lauren Ploch, *Countering Terrorism in East Africa: The U.S. Response*, Washington, D.C.: Congressional Research Service, November 3, 2010.

[32] Christopher S. Stewart, "A Bet on Peace for War-Torn Somalia," *Wall Street Journal*, April 26, 2013.

[33] Author discussions with Kenyan military officials, July 2015.

operations with Somali National Army and AMISOM commandos who conducted raids against al Shabaab camps. Another was the provision of intelligence, surveillance, and reconnaissance to AMISOM countries conducting ground operations, including from U.S. airborne platforms such as the Global Hawk unmanned surveillance aircraft. Yet another was U.S. airstrikes, which targeted al Shabaab operatives. In 2015 alone, U.S. strikes killed more than 100 rank-and-file al Shabaab fighters, particularly during such campaigns as Operation Jubba Corridor. As DoD press secretary Peter Cook remarked following a U.S. strike, "the United States will continue to use the tools at our disposal—financial, diplomatic, and military—to dismantle al Shabaab."[34]

While the number of U.S. strikes was relatively low compared with those in such countries as Iraq, Syria, and Afghanistan, U.S. strikes were precise and effective, killing several key senior al Shabaab leaders. In September 2014, a U.S. strike in Dahay Tubaako, a remote area in Somalia's Lower Shabelle region, killed Ahmed Abdi Godane (aka Mukhtar Abu Zubayr), al Shabaab's leader. In March 2015, Adan Garaar, believed to be the head of Amniyat's external operations, was killed in a U.S. strike in Baardheere. Garaar was assessed to be a leading planner of the September 2013 Westgate attack. Other prominent individuals killed included Sahal Iskudhuq, a senior Amniyat commander, in January 2014; Tahlil Abdishakur, an Amniyat commander, in December 2014; and Yusuf Dheeq, a senior Amniyat member, in January 2015.[35] In December 2015, a U.S. strike killed Abdirahman

---

[34] U.S. Department of Defense, "Statement from Pentagon Press Secretary Peter Cook on December 2 Airstrike in Somalia," Release No: NR-462-15, Washington, D.C., December 7, 2015.

[35] Data in this paragraph come U.S. Department of Defense sources such as Terri Moon Cronk, "DoD Confirms U.S. Strikes Killed Senior Terrorist Operatives," U.S. Department of Defense, December 7, 2015; U.S. Department of Defense, 2015; Nick Simeone, "U.S. Conducts Counterterrorism Operations in Somalia," U.S. Department of Defense, March 13, 2015; Cheryl Pellerin, "U.S. Attack Kills Key al-Shabaab Operative in Somalia," U.S. Department of Defense, March 18, 2015; "Department of Defense Press Briefing by Rear Adm. Kirby in the Pentagon Briefing Room," News Transcript Press Operations, U.S. Department of Defense, February 3, 2015; U.S. Department of Defense, "Statement by Pentagon Press Secretary Rear Adm. John Kirby on Today's Airstrike in Somalia," Release No.:

Sandhere (also known as "Ukash"), prompting one DoD official to note that "Ukash's removal from the battlefield is a significant blow to al Shabaab."[36] One of the largest U.S. strikes occurred in March 2016, when U.S. aircraft targeted al Shabaab's Raso training camp, killing roughly 170 al Shabaab fighters.[37] Following the March strike, the United States pursued an aggressive targeting campaign against al Shabaab operatives in such areas as Lower Jubba and Lower Shabelle.

These strikes need to be viewed in context. Decapitation strategies—which involve attempting to destroy a group by eliminating its leadership—alone are insufficient to defeat most terrorist and insurgent groups. But targeting terrorist and insurgent leaders is an effective, perhaps essential, element of a broader strategy. This is what made U.S. targeting in Somalia so effective: It was embedded in a broader strategy that involved building partner capacity and direct action.[38] U.S. strikes appeared to weaken al Shabaab in several ways. They disrupted al Shabaab strategy and operations by taking off the battlefield key leaders (such as Ahmed Abdi Godane) and operatives (such as Amniyat leaders like Adan Garaar, who were involved in planning operations). In addition, strikes against dug-in al Shabaab positions

---

NR-633-14, December 29, 2014; "Pentagon Confirms Death of al-Shabab Co-Founder," U.S. Department of Defense, September 5, 2014; Claudette Roulo, "Somalia Airstrike Targeted Al-Shabab Leader, Camp, Official Says," U.S. Department of Defense, September 2, 2014; U.S. Department of Defense, "Department of Defense Press Briefing by Rear Adm. Kirby in the Pentagon Briefing Room," News Transcript Press Operations, September 2, 2014. Also see Craig Whitlock and Kevin Sieff, "U.S. Launches Drone Strike Against al Shabab Figure Tied to Kenya Mall Attack," *Washington Post*, March 13, 2015; Helene Cooper, "Pentagon Confirms Strike Killed Shabab Militant Leader in Somalia," *New York Times*, March 18, 2015; Andrew McGregor, "After Garissa: Kenya Revises Its Security Strategy to Counter al-Shabaab's Shifting Tactics," *Terrorism Monitor*, Vol. 13, No. 8, April 2015; Sunguta West, "Shaykh Ahmad Umar Takes the Helm of Al Shabaab," *Militant Leadership Monitor*, April 2015, p. 4; Lolita C. Baldor, "Officials: U.S. Airstrike Kills Al-Shabaab Leader," Associated Press, February 3, 2015; Associated Press, "Airstrike Is Said to Kill Shabab Figure," *New York Times*, January 26, 2014.

[36] U.S. Department of Defense, 2015.

[37] U.S. Department of Defense, "Statement from Pentagon Press Secretary Peter Cook on Airstrike in Somalia," Release No: NR-076-16, March 7, 2016.

[38] Cronin, 2009, pp. 13–34.

during Operation Jubba Corridor undermined the group's ability to resist AMISOM offensive operations. This allowed Kenyan and Ethiopian forces to clear Diinsoor and Baardheere in July 2015 with limited al Shabaab resistance, since its fighters withdrew to the Jubba River Valley and other areas. More broadly, there is some evidence that targeting insurgent leaders through drone and other airstrikes reduces the ability of groups to operate in a cohesive, efficient manner and limits their ability to control local areas. It also undermines the effectiveness of militant groups by taking off the battlefield individuals with valuable skills, resources, and connections.[39]

Third, the United States helped coordinate AMISOM efforts, including by helping synchronize operations with AMISOM chiefs of defense. During such operations as Eagle, Indian Ocean, and Jubba Corridor, successive U.S. military officials from Combined Joint Task Force–Horn of Africa (CJTF–HOA) shuttled between AMISOM capitals to help plan joint operations and offer assistance. In addition, CJTF-HOA's integration of foreign liaison officers from AMISOM and other countries into its headquarters in Djibouti facilitated political, military, and intelligence coordination.[40]

Other Factors

A range of other factors outside of U.S. and AMISOM control also weakened al Shabaab. One was the war in Iraq and Syria, which attracted a growing number of Somalia diaspora fighters away from Somalia and toward the Iraq and Syria battlefields. In April 2015, for example, six Somali Americans from Minneapolis were arrested

---

[39] Patrick B. Johnston, "Does Decapitation Work? Assessing the Effectiveness of Leadership Targeting in Counterinsurgency Campaigns," *International Security*, Vol. 36, No. 4, Spring 2012, pp. 47–79. For contrarian views, see, for example, Jenna Jordan, "Attacking the Leader, Missing the Mark: What Terrorist Groups Survive Decapitation Strikes," *International Security*, Vol. 38, No. 4, Spring 2014, pp. 7–38; Jenna Jordan, "When Heads Roll: Assessing the Effectiveness of Leadership Decapitation," *Security Studies*, Vol. 18, No. 4, 2009, pp. 719–755.

[40] Wayne W. Grigsby, Jr., Todd Fox, Matthew F. Dabkowski, and Andrea N. Phelps, "Globally Integrated Operations in the Horn of Africa Through Principles of Mission Command," *Military Review*, Vol. 95, No. 5, September–October 2015, pp. 9–18.

for providing material support and resources to—and attempting to join—the Islamic State.[41] According to Richard T. Thornton, head of the Federal Bureau of Investigation's field office in Minnesota, Somalis in that state who were once inspired to join al Shabaab in Somalia were increasingly drawn to the Islamic State.[42] Indeed, a number of radicalized Americans from East African countries supported the Islamic State.[43] The decrease in foreign fighter flows to Somalia severely constricted a once-important recruitment pool for al Shabaab.[44]

A second related factor was internal divisions over support to the Islamic State. Al Shabaab's leadership had become increasingly fractured long before the rise of the Islamic State, with competition and discussion between Ahmed Abdi Godane, who embraced the global jihad and eschewed Somalia's clan structure, and Mukhtar Robow, who was a more traditional Somali clan figure. The rift threatened to split the group when it merged with al Qa'ida. The duel between al Qa'ida and the Islamic State seems to have exacerbated this leadership struggle.

It was troubling enough for al Shabaab that foreign fighters increasingly traveled to battlefields in the Middle East, rather than to Somalia. But it was doubly difficult when some members of al Shabaab lobbied to join the Islamic State and split with al Qa'ida. In October 2015, for instance, senior al Shabaab member Abud Qadr Mu'min and nearly two dozen of his followers pledged support to the Islamic State, causing internal fissures.[45] An audio message attributed to Mu'min stated that "we the mujahideen of Somalia announce our pledge of

---

[41] United States District Court for the District of Minnesota, *United States of America v. Mohamed Abdihamid Farah, Adnan Abdihamid Farah, Abdurahman Yasin Daud, Zacharia Yusuf Abdurahman, Hanad Mustafe Musse, and Guled Ali Omar*, Criminal Complaint, April 18, 2015.

[42] "We Have a Terror Recruiting Problem in Minnesota," CBS News, April 20, 2015.

[43] Fordham Law School, *By the Numbers: ISIS Cases in the United States, March 1, 2014–June 22, 2015*, New York: Center on National Security at Fordham Law, June 25, 2015.

[44] Committee on Homeland Security, 2011.

[45] "Shabaab Arrests Fighters Pledged to IS," SITE Intelligence Group, October 2015; "Jihadists Give Conflicting Reports of Coming Clashes Between Shabaab and Pro-IS Defectors," SITE Intelligence Group, October 2015; "Shabaab Fighters' Pledges to IS Prompts Disputes

allegiance to the Caliph," Abu Bakr al-Baghdadi.[46] But al Shabaab and its allies quickly responded. As a public statement by the pro–al Shabaab group Al-Muhajiroun noted, "For many months there has been a redundant debate within East Africa and beyond concerning the pledging of Baya'ah to those far afield." The group then expressed regret about the "unhelpful pronouncement of a minority of individuals and their so-called Baya'ah" to the Islamic State.[47] The internal divisions within al Shabaab came at an inauspicious time, just as the group was at its lowest point in territorial control in several years.

A third factor included al Shabaab's mistakes during the East African drought in 2011 and 2012, which undermined its support base. The resulting famine was particularly devastating in Somalia.[48] On November 11, 2011, al Shabaab announced that it was banning numerous international organizations and NGOs from operating in its areas of operation, such as the World Health Organization and the UN. Al Shabaab accused these organizations of misappropriating funds, promoting secularism and democratic values, and working with church groups to convert Muslim children to Christianity. It accused the UN's Political Office for Somalia of acting "as an impediment to the attainment of lasting peace and stability in the country" and attempting to "foment dissent and ill-will among the local tribes, thereby keeping the Somali state in a perpetual cycle of conflict and disharmony."[49] In response, al Shabaab also set up the Office for Supervising the Affairs of Foreign Agencies to monitor the limited humanitarian assistance that remained. The UN reported that famine killed more than a quar-

Among Jihadists, Unanimous Prediction of Bloodshed," SITE Intelligence Group, October 2015.

[46] Audio message by Abdul Qadr Mu'min, distributed on Twitter and pro-ISIS Telegram channels, October 22, 2015.

[47] "Hold Fast, Together," Al-Muhajiroun–Emigrants of East Africa, October 24, 2015.

[48] Menkhaus, 2014.

[49] Al Shabaab, "Somali Population Must be Wary of Illegitimate Organizations Such as UNPOS," *Al-Kataib Foundation for Media Productions,* January 2012.

ter million Somalis, half of them children, between October 2010 and April 2012.[50]

Al Shabaab's reputation suffered markedly, and the decision to ban humanitarian aid organizations was a public-relations nightmare. As one study concluded, al Shabaab's conduct "towards those providing desperately needed aid has turned many who previously supported them against the group. It also occasioned a split within the group."[51]

Conclusion

By 2016, al Shabaab lost much of the territory it once controlled following a series of AMISOM offensives such as Operation Linda Nchi (2011), Operation Sledge Hammer (2012), Operation Eagle (2014), Operation Indian Ocean (2014), and Operation Jubba Corridor (2015). The United States and other Western countries supported these efforts by conducting direct action operations that targeted al Shabaab's leadership; training, advising, and assisting AMISOM countries, the Somali National Army, and Somalia clan militias; and helping coordinate AMISOM activities. In addition, al Shabaab faced growing internal dissension that increased defections within the organization, and its leaders made several serious miscalculations during the drought.

The tailored engagement strategy of the United States, which combined local ground forces with precision strikes and training from U.S. special operations and intelligence forces, was more successful than previous efforts in Somalia in contributing to the loss of al Shabaab territory, finances, cohesion, and recruits. The relatively large U.S. footprint and robust intervention strategy in the early 1990s, which reached 5.7 U.S. and other foreign troops per 1,000 Somali inhabitants in 1992, triggered widespread opposition to foreign intervention. The indirect engagement strategy and 2006 Ethiopian military invasion of Somalia also contributed to a significant religious and national-

---

[50] "Somalia Famine Killed Nearly 260,000 People, Half of Them Children, Reports UN," United Nations News Centre, May 2, 2013.

[51] Atwan, 2012, p. 118.

ist backlash, which contributed to the rise of al Shabaab. This tailored engagement strategy has important implications for U.S. counterterrorism and counterinsurgency operations in other areas of the world.

As the next chapter highlights, a mix of challenges and opportunities remain in Somalia. Al Shabaab has not been eliminated, and it remains capable of conducting terrorist attacks in Somalia and the region. AMISOM countries continue to be plagued by limited political will, delayed operations, coordination problems, and logistics and manpower shortfalls. Somalia itself faces substantial political, economic, security, and governance challenges that remain largely unaddressed.

CHAPTER FOUR
Recommendations

Al Shabaab evolved from one of several militant groups in Somalia to a powerful insurgent organization that governed roughly half of Somalia and, more recently, to a terrorist group that lost most of the territory it once controlled. The tailored engagement strategy outlined in Chapter Three was relatively successful in undermining al Shabaab's territorial control, finances, cohesion, and recruits—at least temporarily. This chapter assesses the difficult road ahead by focusing on how to expand on recent progress. Like most efforts against a terrorist or insurgent group, the struggle is primarily *political*, not military.[1] Consequently, the political and related social, economic, and governance efforts in Somalia will largely determine whether recent successes lead to a country that is more stable and prevent the resurgence of al Shabaab or other militant groups. Since the early 1990s, Somalia has lacked a functioning state capable of enforcing law and order or delivering services. German sociologist Max Weber defined the state as "a human community that (successfully) claims the monopoly of the legitimate use of physical force within a given territory."[2] In the absence of a functioning central government, it will be difficult to sustain the military advances in Somalia.

Lacking persistent efforts against al Shabaab, the progress over the past several years is reversible. Al Shabaab retains several seasoned

---

[1] On the importance of politics in insurgent warfare see, for example, Mao, 2000.

[2] Max Weber, "Politics as a Vocation," in H. H. Gerth and C. Wright Mills, eds., *From Max Weber: Essays in Sociology*, New York: Oxford University Press, 1958, p. 78.

operatives, such as emir Ahmed Diriye, chief of Amniyat Habil al-Somali, and senior official Mahad Karate. It has used a suite of assassinations, raids, kidnappings, and bombings to coerce local populations. Al Shabaab has also appointed a range of new governors, trained administrators, adjudicated disputes in its courts, broadcast government failures, and publicized aid delivery in an effort to improve its governance capacity and regain territory.[3] Military successes on the battlefield are transitory and cannot fix the political and other grievances ailing Somalia. Iraq is a useful example. In 2011, for example, al Qa'ida in Iraq was in decline. The group had lost control over most of the territory it once controlled, and the population of key provinces such as al Anbar had turned against it. Much as with al Shabaab, al Qa'ida in Iraq was too brutal, controlling, incompetent at governance, and prone to infighting. Still, a combination of factors—political, economic, and even military—contributed to al Qa'ida in Iraq's return as the Islamic State in 2014.

Any policy recommendations for Somalia must acknowledge the complexity of the local landscape, including the clan dynamics. Somalia's history conspires against optimism. What makes this moment in Somalia possibly different than others before? There are two factors. First, the extent to which al Shabaab has been weakened, at least for the moment, is different than in prior years. There may have been opportunities in previous periods, such as after the collapse of the ICU in 2007, but international support was limited. A second factor is the coalition cooperating against extremists. The United States, European Union, AMISOM (particularly the involvement of Somalia's strongest neighbors, Kenya and Ethiopia), and a slightly more united and committed Somali government provide a window of opportunity for action. These two factors allow for an increased chance to pursue a holistic approach to Somali policy, incorporating critical external support and assistance but infusing a local, Somali character and centered on Somali ownership of their own problems. Policymakers in these countries need to exploit the military successes and continue momentum. There are

---

[3] On al Shabaab's resiliency see Christopher Anzalone, "The Resilience of al-Shabaab," *CTC Sentinel*, Vol. 9, No. 4, April 2016, pp. 13–20.

five interlinked and concurrent lines of effort that U.S. policymakers should consider.

Reopen the U.S. embassy. Statements of support from Washington are important, as are periodic visits from senior U.S. government officials to Mogadishu. But a permanent presence is critical for U.S. diplomats to understand the shifting dynamics in Somalia, develop strong relations with Somalia's leaders, participate in peace discussions, exert U.S. influence in the region, and oversee development efforts led by such organizations as the U.S. Agency for International Development (USAID). Local officials need a local address to engage with Americans. The lack of a permanent U.S. State Department presence in Somalia—particularly an embassy—undermines U.S. efforts to build on the recent successes against al Shabaab. The United States closed its embassy in 1991 during the Somali civil war, when the USS *Guam* and USS *Trenton*, which were stationed off the coast of Oman, were dispatched to airlift staff from the embassy in Mogadishu. But security concerns and the lingering political fear of another Benghazi incident, which led to the death of U.S. Ambassador Christopher Stevens and three other Americans, have hamstrung America's political response in Somalia. It is noteworthy that several of America's North Atlantic Treaty Organization (NATO) allies—including the United Kingdom and Turkey—have embassies in Somalia.

Increase economic assistance. Revitalizing America's diplomatic presence in Somalia can have important second- and third-order effects, including more-targeted and effective economic programs through such organizations as USAID. There was virtually no follow-on development assistance once AMISOM forces cleared Diinsoor and Baardheere in July 2015, an unfortunate development. Most successful counterinsurgency campaigns have required political, economic, and social programs to help fill the vacuum once military forces clear territory. Famine, drought, the destruction of infrastructure, and decades of neglect leave Somalia dependent on foreign aid, the lack of which could unravel progress on the ground as local communities look to whoever can pull them out of desperate poverty. Somalis are coming back to Somalia. It is encouraging to see an uptick in commercial flights arriving in Mogadishu with diaspora Somalis. They bring resources, money, and hope to the country. But Somalia will need outside assistance as well. This does not mean large amounts of money, since the Somali government cannot absorb a large influx of aid. Still, targeted economic assistance in areas liberated from al Shabaab, particularly in southern and central Somalia, is important to ensure that these areas do not fall back into al Shabaab's hands.

Augment U.S. military train, advise, assist, and accompany efforts. One of the most significant challenges with a tailored engagement strategy is the competence and political will of local partners. Somali National Army forces are weak and poorly trained, and AMISOM countries have frequently turned to clan militias to help fill the political and security vacuums following al Shabaab's withdrawal. With help from the United States and other partners, Somalia developed the Guulwade ("Victory") Plan. The plan outlines the Somali National Army's arms and equipment needs for improved joint operations and offers a framework to train and equip 10,900 national army troops. But Mogadishu has lacked the political will to adequately implement the Guulwade Plan. AMISOM forces might be able to take ground, but Somalis have to hold it over the long run.

U.S. military assistance to the Somali National Army has been limited and incremental, which is unfortunate, since the army is a critical component of long-term stability. As part of a more effective tailored engagement strategy, the United States needs to train, advise, assist, and occasionally accompany Somali forces out in the field, as well as helping develop the capacity of the Ministry of Defense and Ministry of Interior. Since clans and other substate actors are a reality in Somalia—and will be for the foreseeable future—the United States also needs to better understand Somalia's complex clan structure and the key local powerbrokers. Thus far, however, Mogadishu has made scant progress in professionalizing nonstate militias and integrating them into, or coordinating them better with, the Somali National Army.

Aid Somalia's neighbors and support continuation of AMISOM. Troop-contributing countries such as Ethiopia, Kenya, Burundi, Cameroon, Djibouti, and Uganda need to continue playing an important role in countering al Shabaab politically, economically, socially, and militarily. During the mid-2000s, Somalis strongly rejected Ethiopia's unilateral operations in the country, which contributed to the rise of al Shabaab. But conducting operations through a regional organization such as AMISOM, the efforts have been far more palatable for the Somali population, according to some public opinion polls.[4] Troop-contributing countries have various motives for cooperating in Somalia. Some, such as Ethiopia and Kenya, see al Shabaab and its attacks as a direct threat to their security. Each of these countries needs U.S. and other Western training, advice, and assistance in Somalia. As noted in Chapter Three, U.S. aid to the Kenyan Defense Forces during Operational Jubba Corridor was critical in helping clear Baardheere in July 2015.

Each of these AMISOM countries also has challenges. Ethiopia's human rights record is poor, including its crackdown on political dissent.[5] Uganda and Burundi have been accused, rightly or wrongly, of sending forces to AMISOM for financial reasons. AMISOM countries also failed to follow up on their military successes in 2015 with aggressive operations against al Shabaab in 2016 in the Jubba River region, particularly north of Jilib and south of Baardheere in southern Somalia. Still, the United States needs to maintain support for these AMISOM countries, which is fairly inexpensive. A withdrawal of their support—particularly Somalia's neighbors—would severely undermine efforts to stabilize Somalia.

Continue limited U.S. direct action operations. The United States has unique intelligence and precision-strike capabilities to target the leaders of terrorist and insurgent groups. The United States should continue to support a few hundred military personnel, including logistics support, to conduct direct action operations against al Shabaab as part of a tailored engagement strategy. The urgency of other priorities, including against Islamic State leaders in Iraq and Syria, should not strip the deployment of special operations forces; legal authorities; or

---

[4]   See, for example, the poll by ORB International cited in David Ochami and Peter Opiyo, "More Somalis Support Foreign Efforts, Says Poll," *The Standard*, March 26, 2012.

[5]   See, for example, Human Rights Watch, *World Report 2015: Ethiopia*, New York: Human Rights Watch, 2015.

intelligence, surveillance, and reconnaissance platforms to take lethal action against al Shabaab leaders.

Despite progress against al Shabaab, the situation in Somalia is fragile. The United States and other Western governments have committed insufficient few resources and attention to addressing Somalia's political, economic, and governance challenges at the heart of the conflict. It is time to reconsider before this fleeting window of opportunity is lost.-

Appendix

Table A.1
Example of al Shabaab Senior Leadership Deaths and Detentions

Name of Deceased/Detainee	Leadership Role(s)	Month/Year Killed or Detained
Abdullahi Sudi Arale	al Shabaab political leader	January 2007
Sheikh Abdullahi Mo'alim Ali 'Abu Utayba'	al Shabaab senior official	January 2007
Abu Talha al Sudani	al Qa'ida operative in East Africa	May 2008
Aden Hashi Ayro	al Shabaab cofounder and commander; al Qa'ida operative in East Africa	May 2008
Sheikh Muhyadin Omar	al Shabaab senior official	May 2008
Saleh Ali Saleh Nabhan	al Qa'ida operative in East Africa	September 2009
Mukhtar Robow Ali	al Shabaab cofounder, spokesman	June 2010
Abdullah Fazul (aka Fazul Mohammed)	Head of East Africa al Qa'ida (EAAQ); ICU intelligence chief	June 2011
Bilal al Berjawi (aka Abu Hafsa)	al Qa'ida operative in East Africa	January 2012
Ibrahim al-Afghani	al Shabaab cofounder; First Afghan War vet; AIAI commander	June 2013
Abul Hamid Hash Olhayi (aka Maa'lim Hash)	al Shabaab cofounder	June 2013
Hassan Dahir Aweys	al Shabaab cofounder	August 2013
Shaykh Muktar Robow	al Shabaab cofounder	August 2013

Table A.1—Continued

Name of Deceased/Detainee	Leadership Role(s)	Month/Year Killed or Detained
Omar Hammami (aka Abu Mansur al-Amriki)	al Shabaab spokesman	September 2013
Abdullahi Ali (aka Ante Ante)	al Shabaab commanders	October 2013
Two unidentified military commanders	al Shabaab commander	October 2013
Ahmed Mohamed Amey	al Shabaab senior official	January 2014
Ahmed Abdi Godane (aka Mukhtar Abu Zubayr)	al Shabaab emir, cofounder	September 2014
Abdishakur (aka Tahlil)	al Shabaab's chief of security and intelligence wing (Amniyaat)	December 2014
Sahal Iskudhuq	al Shabaab senior intelligence officer	January 2015
Yusef Dheeq	Abdishakur's successor as al Shabaab's chief of security and intelligence wing (Amniyaat)	January 2015
Olow Barow	al Shabaab military commander	February 2015
Adan Garar	al Shabaab senior official	March 2015
Hassan Turki	ICU founder, al Shabaab leader, first Afghan War veteran, AIAI leader, leader of Ras Kamboni Brigade	May 2015
Abdirahman Sandhere (aka Ukash)	al Shabaab senior official	December 2015
Hassan Ali Dhoore	al Shabaab senior official	March 2016
Abdullahi Haji Da'ud	al Shabaab senior official	May 2016

Table A.2
Chronology of International Advisory/Assistance and Joint Military
Missions in Somalia and Kenya, 1992–2016

Date Start–Date End	Mission Name	Mandate
April 1992–March 1993	UNOSOM I	Ceasefire monitoring in Mogadishu; protection of humanitarian convoys in Mogadishu (later expanded to protection of convoys outside of Mogadishu)
March 1993–March 1995	UNOSOM II	Mandate expanded to allow enforcement measures to improve security for humanitarian convoys throughout Somalia, including disarmament, demobilization, and reintegration operations
February 2007–July 2010	African Union Mission in Somalia I (AMISOM I)	Initially mandated as a regional *peacekeeping* force approved to support the TFG
July 2010–early 2012	African Union Mission in Somalia II (AMISOM II)	Mission expanded in July 2010 from peacekeeping to peace *enforcement*
Early 2012–present	African Union Mission in Somalia III (AMISOM III)	Mission expanded again in early 2012 to allow operations outside Mogadishu, reinforcements from Sierra Leone and Djibouti

Data Collection Sources and Notes

Collecting consistent and reliable open-source data on terrorist and insurgent attacks in such war zones as Somalia—where ungoverned territories are vast, media presence is restricted, and communications infrastructure is archaic—is difficult. Recognizing this reality, we examined and compared three publicly available data sets to best assess trends in al Shabaab violence: the Global Terrorism Database, hosted by START at the University of Maryland; ACLED, supported by the Climate Change and African Political Stability Project at the University of Texas at Austin; and the Terrorism Events Database maintained by IHS Jane's Terrorism and Insurgency Centre. Based on our assessment of sources and coding, we relied on START and ACLED data in the text of the document.

Still, the general trends were similar across these databases. Al Shabaab–initiated attacks rose most every year despite AMISOM and allied successes in regaining territory, although year-specific data sometimes diverged significantly between START, ACLED, and Jane's. The reason for these differences seems to be a matter of sources, rather than of coding methods or definitions. For instance, in 2014, START recorded 864 attacks, close to the 1,081 recorded by ACLED. In 2015, however, START recorded just 384 attacks (a 55-percent decline), while ACLED recorded 910 attacks (a 16-percent decline). According to START coders we contacted, the decline in al Shabaab attacks in their database was attributable to the discontinuation of one key source. In 2014, START researchers had access to Special Operations Command Africa's "Al-Shabaab Incident Tracker" through the Open Source Center, but in 2015, they did not.

In contrast, ACLED maintained access to an embedded Somali network of local reporters who released daily information on the status of political instability in the country. Their data set consistently recorded more events than either START's or Jane's databases. However, because of the need to protect their sources, ACLED's data set lacks transparency. ACLED attributed the majority of attacks to the "Local Source Project," which we could not independently verify.

We also examined another source of attack data: al Shabaab claims of responsibility. Since August 2015, al Shabaab published monthly incident-report summaries, which were then translated and reproduced by the SITE Intelligence Group. The number of attacks in these monthly roundups ranged from 50 to 80 per edition in the seven-month period from August 2015 to March 2016. Extrapolating these figures, a reasonable estimate of the number of annual attacks in 2015 and 2016 might thus range from 600 to 1,000.

Finally, there are several aspects of data uncertainty. First, a vast number of incidents are coded as involving "unknown perpetrators" for all three data sets. For instance, ACLED records the following number of events in Somalia involving "unidentified armed groups" from 2007 to 2015: 2007 (623), 2008 (531), 2009 (316), 2010 (338), 2011 (346),

2012 (685), 2013 (1148), 2014 (835), and 2015 (546). The number of recorded events involving "unknown groups" is less dramatic in the START database but still significant relative to the number of al Shabaab events: 2007 (130), 2008 (129), 2009 (53), 2010 (51), 2011 (51), 2012 (136), 2013 (55), and 2014 (80). Not all of these events likely involved al Shabaab fighters, but some may have. Consequently, it is possible that the number of al Shabaab attacks and fatalities reported by these sources is a conservative estimate and understated total numbers, particularly in the early years of al Shabaab's existence.

Second, ACLED included a larger number of conflict events than the START or Jane's databases, perhaps because of its embedded network of local Somali journalists. This repository included a variety of acts of violence committed by—and against—al Shabaab forces. In reviewing the ACLED data set, we attempted to isolate only incidents initiated by al Shabaab. In the majority of cases, the descriptions provided in the ACLED data set made this coding straightforward and included such acts as assassinations, torture and mutilations, beheadings, improvised explosive devices, mortar and grenade attacks, hit-and-run attacks, ambushes, raids, bombings, suicide attacks, shootings, destruction of infrastructure and religious artifacts, kidnappings, hostage takings, and forced recruitment of civilians. We included these incidents.

The ACLED data set also included a large number of attacks and other events *against* al Shabaab forces, which were initiated by government forces or nonstate groups. Examples included U.S. strikes, Kenyan airstrikes, AMISOM raids and arrests, Somali government–led military offensives and security operations, government mortar strikes, and battles initiated by other nonstate groups. We excluded these events, even if they elicited a violent al Shabaab response such as sustained gunfights or heavy retaliatory shelling. For instance, if an ACLED incident description reported that transitional government forces initiated an offensive operation by entering a village controlled by al Shabaab and heavy clashes followed, we excluded such an event.

We also observed a limited number of incidents in which the description provided by the ACLED data set was insufficient to determine whether the event was initiated by al Shabaab or by government forces or nonstate actors. For instance, an incident description might ambiguously indicate that heavy fighting occurred between al Shabaab and AMISOM forces in a certain village on a certain date. Or it might indicate that heavy shelling or mortar exchanges were reported between both sides in a city such as Mogadishu on a given day. But we could not determine from the ACLED event summary which group instigated the incident of violence. As a coding rule, we included such events in our data count, but for transparency's sake, we coded them distinctly. Because of this coding decision, the annual totals of al Shabaab–initiated attacks might be slightly overstated in some years. The ambiguous events are: 2008 (68), 2009 (34), 2010 (246), 2011 (69), 2012 (114), 2013 (67), 2014 (76), and 2015 (65).

About the Authors

Seth G. Jones is director of the International Security and Defense Policy Center at the RAND Corporation, as well as an adjunct professor at the School for Advanced International Studies at Johns Hopkins University. He served as the representative for the commander, U.S. Special Operations Command, to the Assistant Secretary of Defense for Special Operations. Before that, he served as a plans officer and advisor to the commanding general, U.S. Special Operations Forces, in Afghanistan (Combined Forces Special Operations Component Command–Afghanistan). Jones specializes in counterinsurgency and counterterrorism, including a focus on al Qa'ida and ISIS/ISIL. He is the author of *Waging Insurgent Warfare* (Oxford University Press, forthcoming), *Hunting in the Shadows: The Pursuit of al Qa'ida after 9/11* (W. W. Norton, 2012), *In the Graveyard of Empires: America's War in Afghanistan* (W. W. Norton, 2009), and *The Rise of European Security Cooperation* (Cambridge University Press, 2007). Jones has published articles in a range of journals, such as *Foreign Affairs, Foreign Policy,* and *International Security,* as well as in such newspapers and magazines as the *New York Times, Washington Post,* and *Wall Street Journal.* Jones received his M.A. and Ph.D. from the University of Chicago.

Andrew M. Liepman is a senior policy analyst at the RAND Corporation. He retired in August 2012 as the Principal Deputy Director of the National Counterterrorism Center (NCTC) after a career of more than 30 years in the U.S. Central Intelligence Agency (CIA). He spent much of his career on Middle East and terrorism issues. He served for three years at the U.S. Department of State and in a variety of Intelligence Community assignments, including positions in the Nonproliferation Center and the National Intelligence Council. Liepman was the Deputy Chief of CIA's Office of Near East and South Asian Analysis; the Deputy Director of the Office of Weapons Intelligence, Arms Control, and Nonproliferation; the Chief of the Office of Iraq Analysis; and the Deputy Chief of CIA's Counterterrorism Center. Prior to joining RAND, he served in the Office of the Director of National Intelligence, first as the Deputy Director of NCTC for Intelligence and then as the Principal Deputy. Liepman earned a B.S. from the University of California, Berkeley.

Nathan Chandler is a project associate at the RAND Corporation, where his recent work focused on counterinsurgency, counterterrorism, and counternarcotics theory and conduct. Prior to rejoining RAND in 2012, Chandler served as a research assistant and course assistant at the Belfer Center for Science and International Affairs at the John F. Kennedy School of Government at Harvard University. From 2006 to 2008, he was as an administrative assistant within RAND's National Security Research Division. Previously, Chandler worked as an intern to U.S. Senator Joseph Lieberman and to U.S. Congresswoman Denise Majette. He earned a masters of public policy (MPP) in international and global affairs from John F. Kennedy School of Government at Harvard University in 2010 and a B.A. in English literature from Emory University in 2004.

References

al-Afghani, Ibrahim, "Urgent and Open Letter to Our Amiir Shaykh Ayman al-Zawahiri," April 2013. As of May 9, 2016: http://www.somalisecuritystudies.blogspot.no

Ali, Laila, "Somalia: On the Run Again–Somali Refugees Return Home from Yemen," August 28, 2015. As of May 9, 2016: https://www.wfp.org/stories/somali-refugees-yemen

"Ali Dheere: We Targeted the French in Djibouti for Their Massacres in Central Africa," Shahada News Agency, May 27, 2014.

Amble, John C., and Alexander Meleagrou-Hitchens, "*Jihadist* Radicalization in East Africa: Two Case Studies," *Studies in Conflict and Terrorism*, Vol. 37, 2014, pp. 523–540.

"American Officers Killed in a Martyrdom-Seeking Operation on the Outskirts of Mogadishu," Shahada News Agency, March 17, 2014.

"An Exclusive Interview with Sheikh Ali Muhammad Hussein, Governor of Islamic Banaadir Province," Shahada News Agency, July 11, 2014.

Anderson, Noel, "Peacekeepers Fighting a Counterinsurgency Campaign: A Net Assessment of the African Union Mission in Somalia," *Studies in Conflict and Terrorism*, Vol. 37, No. 11, 2014, pp. 936–958.

Anzalone, Christopher, "The Resilience of al-Shabaab," *CTC Sentinel*, Vol. 9, No. 4, April 2016, pp. 13–20. As of July 6, 2016: https://www.ctc.usma.edu/posts/the-resilience-of-al-shabaab

Associated Press, "Final Statement of the Conference of Islamic State Scholars in Somalia," cache of documents found by the Associated Press on the floor in a building occupied by al-Qaida fighters in Timbuktu, Mali, December 3, 2011. As of May 5, 2016: http://hosted.ap.org/specials/interactives/_international/_pdfs/al-qaida-papers-state-scholars.pdf

————, "Airstrike Is Said to Kill Shabab Figure," *New York Times*, January 26, 2014. As of May 9, 2016:
http://www.nytimes.com/2014/01/27/world/africa/airstrike-is-said-to-kill-shabab-figure.html

Atwan, Abdel Bari, *After bin Laden: Al Qaeda, the Next Generation*, New York: The New Press, 2012, p. 113.

Baldor, Lolita C., "Officials: U.S. Airstrike Kills Al-Shabab Leader," Associated Press, February 3, 2015.

BBC News, "Profile: Somalia's Islamic Courts," June 6, 2006. As of May 9, 2016:
http://news.bbc.co.uk/2/hi/africa/5051588.stm

Benjamin, Daniel, and Steven Simon, *The Age of Sacred Terror: Radical Islam's War Against America*, New York: Random House, 2003, pp. 118–123.

Bentley, David, and Robert Oakley, "Peace Operations: A Comparison of Somalia and Haiti," National Defense University, *Strategic Forum*, No. 30, May 1995.

Billow, Abdulaziz, "Somali Refugees Sail Home from Yemen," Voice of America, August 19, 2015. As of May 9, 2016:
http://www.voanews.com/content/somali-refugees-sail-home-from-yemen/2924517.html

Blanchard, Lauren Ploch, *The September 2013 Terrorist Attack in Kenya: In Brief*, Washington, D.C.: Congressional Research Service, November 14, 2013. As of May 9, 2016:
https://www.fas.org/sgp/crs/row/R43245.pdf

Central Intelligence Agency, *Guide to the Analysis of Insurgency*, Washington, D.C., 2012, p. 1.

Chaliand, Gérard, ed., *Guerrilla Strategies: An Historical Anthology from the Long March to Afghanistan*, Berkeley, Calif.: University of California Press, 1982.

Childress, Sarah, "Somalia's Al Shabaab to Ally with Al Qaeda," *Wall Street Journal*, February 2, 2010. As of May 9, 2016:
http://www.wsj.com/articles/SB10001424052748704107204575038674123215854

Clarke, Walter, and Jeffrey Herbst, *Learning from Somalia: The Lessons of Armed Humanitarian Intervention*, Boulder, Colo.: Westview Press, 1997.

Clapper, James R., "Statement for the Record: Worldwide Threat Assessment of the U.S. Intelligence Community," testimony before the Senate Select Committee on Intelligence, February 9, 2016. As of May 5, 2016:
https://www.dni.gov/files/documents/SSCI_Unclassified_2016_ATA_SFR%20_FINAL.pdf

Committee on Homeland Security, *Al Shabaab: Recruitment and Radicalization Within the Muslim American Community and the Threat to the Homeland*, Washington, D.C., Government Printing Office, July 27, 2011, p. 2.

Connable, Ben, and Martin Libicki, *How Insurgencies End*, Santa Monica, Calif.: RAND Corporation, MG-965-MCIA, 2010. As of May 9, 2016: http://www.rand.org/pubs/monographs/MG965.html

Cooper, Helene, "Pentagon Confirms Strike Killed Shabab Militant Leader in Somalia," *New York Times*, March 18, 2015. As of May 9, 2016: http://www.nytimes.com/2015/03/19/us/politics/pentagon-confirms-strike-killed-shabab-militant-leader-in-somalia.html

Council of the European Union, "Somalia: EU Extends Training Mission," March 16, 2015. As of May 9, 2016: http://www.consilium.europa.eu/en/press/press-releases/2015/03/16-eutm-somalia-training-mission/

Cronk, Terri Moon, "DoD Confirms U.S. Strikes Killed Senior Terrorist Operatives," U.S. Department of Defense, December 7, 2015. As of May 9, 2016: http://www.defense.gov/News-Article-View/Article/633252/dod-confirms-us-strikes-killed-senior-terrorist-operatives

Cronin, Audrey Kurth, "Behind the Curve: Globalization and International Terrorism," *International Security*, Vol. 27, No. 3, Winter 2002/2003, p. 33.

———, *How Terrorism Ends: Understanding the Decline and Demise of Terrorist Campaigns*, Princeton, N.J.: Princeton University Press, 2009.

"Department of Defense Press Briefing by Rear Adm. Kirby in the Pentagon Briefing Room," News Transcript Press Operations, U.S. Department of Defense, February 3, 2015. As of May 9, 2016: http://www.defense.gov/News/News-Transcripts/Article/607008

Dobbins, James, Seth G. Jones, Keith Crane, Christopher S. Chivvis, Andrew Radin, F. Stephen Larrabee, Nora Bensahel, Brooke Stearns Lawson, and Benjamin W. Goldsmith, *Europe's Role in Nation-Building: From the Balkans to the Congo*, Santa Monica, Calif.: RAND Corporation, MG-722-RC, 2008. As of May 9, 2016: http://www.rand.org/pubs/monographs/MG722.html

"Ethiopian Troops Formally Join AMISOM Peacekeepers in Somalia," *AMISOM News*, January 2014. As of May 9, 2016: http://amisom-au.org/2014/01/ethiopian-troops-formally-join-amisom-peacekeepers-in-somalia/

European Union External Action, "Factsheet on EUTM Somalia," October 2014.

"The Experience of Our Brothers in Somalia," in *Al-Qaida Papers*, cache of documents found by the Associated Press on the floor in a building occupied by al-Qaida fighters in Timbuktu, Mali, undated. As of May 9, 2016: http://hosted.ap.org/specials/interactives/_international/_pdfs/al-qaida-papers-somalian-brothers.pdf

Fordham Law School, *By the Numbers: ISIS Cases in the United States, March 1, 2014–June 22, 2015*, New York: Center on National Security at Fordham Law, June 25, 2015.

Freedman, Lawrence, *Strategy: A History*, New York: Oxford University Press, 2013, pp. ix–xvi.

"From the Editor," *Gaidi Mtaani*, Dhul Hijra 1434, toleo 4, p. 1.

Gartenstein-Ross, Daveed, "The Strategic Challenge of Somalia's Al-Shabaab: Dimensions of Jihad," *Middle East Quarterly*, Vol. 16, No. 4, Fall 2009, pp. 25–36.

George, Alexander L., and Timothy J. McKeown, "Case Studies and Theories of Organizational Decision Making," in Robert F. Coulam and Richard A. Smith, eds., *Advances in Information Processing in Organizations: A Research Annual*, Vol. II, Greenwich, Conn.: JAI Press, 1985, p. 35.

Global Terrorism Database, "Codebook: Inclusion Criteria and Variables," College Park, Md.: START: A Center of Exellence of the U.S. Department of Homeland Security, June 2015.

Godane, Ahmed Abdi, "Video Statement," February 9, 2012.

Gordon, Michael R., and Mark Mazetti, "U.S. Used Base in Ethiopia to Hunt al Qaeda," *New York Times*, February 23, 2007. As of May 9, 2016: http://www.nytimes.com/2007/02/23/world/africa/23somalia.html

Grigsby, Jr., Wayne W., Todd Fox, Matthew F. Dabkowski, and Andrea N. Phelps, "Globally Integrated Operations in the Horn of Africa Through Principles of Mission Command," *Military Review*, Vol. 95, No. 5, September–October 2015, pp. 9–18.

"Harakat al Shabaab al-Mujahideen," *Jane's World Insurgency and Terrorism,* February 9, 2015.

Hansen, Stig Jarle, *Al-Shabaab in Somalia: The History of a Militant Islamist Group, 2005–2012*, New York: Oxford University Press, 2013.

———, "An In-Depth Look at al-Shabab's Internal Divisions," *CTC Sentinel*, Vol. 7, No. 2, February 2014, pp. 9–12.

Hart, B. H. Liddell, *Strategy: The Indirect Approach*, London: Faber, 1967, p. 335.

Hegghammer, Thomas, "The Rise of Muslim Foreign Fighters: Islam and the Globalization of Jihad," *International Security*, Vol. 35, No. 3, Winter 2010/2011, pp. 53–94.

Hoffman, Bruce, *Inside Terrorism*, 2nd edition, New York: Columbia University Press, 2006, pp. 1–41.

Human Rights Watch, *World Report 2015: Ethiopia*, New York: Human Rights Watch, 2015. As of May 9, 2016: https://www.hrw.org/world-report/2015/country-chapters/ethiopia

International Crisis Group, *Somalia's Islamists*, Africa Report No. 100, Brussels, Belgium: International Crisis Group, 2005.

———, *Counter-Terrorism in Somalia: Losing Hearts and Minds*, Africa Report No. 95, Brussels, Belgium: International Crisis Group, July 2005.

"IS Fighters and Supporters Celebrate Reports of Possible Pledge from Shaba'ab," SITE Intelligence Group, *Western Jihadist Forum Digest*, July 13, 2015.

Jenkins, Brian Michael, *Stray Dogs and Virtual Armies: Radicalization and Recruitment to Jihadist Terrorism in the United States Since 9/11*, Santa Monica, Calif.: RAND Corporation, OP-343-RC, 2011, pp. 12–14. As of May 9, 2016: http://www.rand.org/pubs/occasional_papers/OP343.html

"Jihadists Give Conflicting Reprots of Coming Clashes Between Shabaab and Pro-IS Defectors," SITE Intelligence Group, October 2015.

Johnston, Patrick B., "Does Decapitation Work? Assessing the Effectiveness of Leadership Targeting in Counterinsurgency Campaigns," *International Security*, Vol. 36, No. 4, Spring 2012, pp. 47–79.

Jones, Seth G., *Hunting in the Shadows: The Pursuit of Al Qa'ida Since 9/11*, New York: W. W. Norton, 2012.

Jones, Seth G., and Martin C. Libicki, *How Terrorist Groups End: Lessons for Countering Al Qa'ida*, Santa Monica, Calif.: RAND Corporation, MG-741-1-RC, 2008. As of May 9, 2016: http://www.rand.org/pubs/monographs/MG741-1.html

Jordan, Jenna, "When Heads Roll: Assessing the Effectiveness of Leadership Decapitation," *Security Studies*, Vol. 18, No. 4, 2009, pp. 719–755.

———, "Attacking the Leader, Missing the Mark: What Terrorist Groups Survive Decapitation Strikes," *International Security*, Vol. 38, No. 4, Spring 2014, pp. 7–38.

Kalyvas, Stathis N., *The Logic of Violence in Civil War*, New Haven, Conn.: Yale University Press, May 2006, p. 245.

al-Kata'ib Media Foundation, "From the Frontlines of Honor," posted on jihadist forums on February 2, 2015.

———, "Punish Them Severely in Order to Disperse Those Who Are Behind Them," 11th episode posted on jihadist websites on July 13, 2015.

Kulish, Nicholas, "American Jihadist Is Believed to Have Been Killed by His Former Allies in Somalia," *New York Times*, September 12, 2013. As of May 9, 2016: http://www.nytimes.com/2013/09/13/world/africa/american-jihadist-is-believed-killed-by-ex-allies-in-somalia.html

Lahoud, Nelly, *Beware of Imitators: Al-Qa'ida Through the Lens of Its Confidential Secretary*, West Point, N.Y.: Harmony Program at the Combating Terrorism Center at West Point, 2012.

Lahoud, Nelly, Stuart Caudill, Liam Collins, Gabriel Koehler-Derrick, Don Rassler, and Muhammad al-'Ubaydi, *Letters from Abbottabad: Bin Ladin Sidelined?* West Point, N.Y.: Harmony Program at the Combating Terrorism Center at West Point, 2012.

Laqueur, Walter, *Guerrilla Warfare: A Historical and Critical Study*, New Brunswick, N.J.: Transaction Publishers, 2010.

"Losing Streak–Public Support Fades for al-Shabab," *AMISOM*, September 2011. As of May 9, 2016:
http://amisom-au.org/2011/09/losing-streak-public-support-fades-for-al-shabab/

Mao Tse-Tung, *On Guerrilla Warfare*, Urbana and Chicago, Ill.: University of Illinois Press, 2000.

McGregor, Andrew, "After Garissa: Kenya Revises Its Security Strategy to Counter al-Shabaab's Shifting Tactics," *Terrorism Monitor*, Vol. 13, No. 8, April 2015.

Mearsheimer, John J., *Conventional Deterrence*, Ithaca, N.Y.: Cornell University Press, 1983, pp. 2, 28–29.

———, *The Tragedy of Great Power Politics*, New York: W. W. Norton, 2001.

Menkhaus, Ken, *Somalia: State Collapse and the Threat of Terrorism*, Adelphi Paper 364, New York: Oxford University Press, 2005.

———, "Al-Shabab's Capabilities Post-Westgate," *CTC Sentinel*, March 24, 2014.

al-Muhajir, Zubair, "Yes There Is a Problem—Open Letter From Sheikh Zubayr al-Muhajir to Sheikh Abu al-Zubair," April 18, 2013. As of May 9, 2016: www.somalisecuritystudies.blogspot.no

al-Muhajir, Abu Abdallah, "From the 'Hood' to an Eternal Paradise," *Gaidi Mtaani*, Issue 7, February 2015, pp. 19–24.

Mwangi, Oscar Gakuo, "State Collapse, Al Shabaab, Islamism, and Legitimacy in Somalia," *Politics, Religion and Ideology*, Vol. 13, No. 4, December 2012, pp. 513–527.

National Commission on Terrorist Attacks upon the United States, *The 9/11 Commission Report*, New York: W. W. Norton, 2004, pp. 59–60.

"O Believers, Make Hijra," on the Deep Web jihad forum Shumukh al-Islam on August 7, 2015.

Ochami, David, and Peter Opiyo, "More Somalis Support Foreign Efforts, Says Poll," *The Standard*, March 26, 2012. As of May 9, 2016:
http://www.standardmedia.co.ke/business/article/2000054913/more-somalis-support-foreign-efforts-says-poll

"Officials in Shabaab Faction Give Fatwa Against Targeting Hammami," SITE Intelligence Group, January 15, 2014.

Olson, Jr., Mancur, *The Logic of Collective Action: Public Goods and the Theory of Groups*, Cambridge, Mass.: Harvard University Press, 1965.

Pape, Robert A., *Dying to Win: The Strategic Logic of Suicide Terrorism*, New York: Random House, 2005, p. 9.

Pellerin, Cheryl, "U.S. Attack Kills Key al-Shabaab Operative in Somalia," U.S. Department of Defense, March 18, 2015. As of May 9, 2016: http://archive.defense.gov/news/newsarticle.aspx?id=128396

"Pentagon Confirms Death of al-Shabab Co-Founder," U.S. Department of Defense, September 5, 2014. As of May 9, 2016: http://www.defense.gov/News-Article-View/Article/603193

Ploch, Lauren, *Countering Terrorism in East Africa: The U.S. Response*, Washington, D.C.: Congressional Research Service, November 3, 2010. As of May 9, 2016: https://www.fas.org/sgp/crs/terror/R41473.pdf

Posen, Barry R., *The Sources of Military Doctrine: France, Britain, and Germany Between the World Wars*, Ithaca, N.Y.: Cornell University Press, 1984, p. 13.

Rage, Sheikh Ali Muhammed, "Public Statement," Shabelle Media Network, October 17, 2011.

———, public statement, News24, November 16, 2011.

Raghavan, Sudarsan, "Kenyan Military Says It Has Driven Al-Shabab Militia from Its Last Stronghold in Somalia," *Washington Post*, September 28, 2012. As of May 9, 2016: https://www.washingtonpost.com/world/africa/kenyan-military-drives-al-qaedas-shabab-militia-out-of-somali-port/2012/09/28/e06b2646-095f-11e2-858a-5311df86ab04_story.html

Rasmussen, Nicholas J., "Hearing Before the Senate Select Committee on Intelligence: Current Terrorist Threat to the United States," February 12, 2015, p. 7. As of May 5, 2016: https://www.dni.gov/index.php/newsroom/testimonies/209-congressional-testimonies-2015/1173-national-counterterrorism-center-director-nicholas-j-rasmussen-statement-for-the-record-before-the-ssci

Roble, Muhyadin Ahmed, "Al-Shabaab: On the Back Foot But Still Dangerous," *Militant Leadership Monitor*, Vol. 13, No. 2, April 2015, p. 2.

Robinson, Linda, "The Future of Special Operations: Beyond Kill and Capture," *Foreign Affairs*, Vol. 91, No. 6, November/December 2012.

———, *The Future of U.S. Special Operations Forces*, New York: Council on Foreign Relations, 2013.

Robow, Mukhtar, "The Martyrdom Night in Barawe [and What Happened] Before and After It," audio recording, September 19, 2013. As of May 9, 2016: www.cunaabi.com/playaudio.php?id=395

Rosen, Armin, "How Africa's Most Threatening Terrorist Group Lost Control of Somalia," *Atlantic*, September 21, 2012. As of May 9, 2016: http://www.theatlantic.com/international/archive/2012/09/how-africas-most-threatening-terrorist-group-lost-control-of-somalia/262655/

Roulo, Claudette, "Somalia Airstrike Targeted al-Shabab Leader, Camp, Official Says," U.S. Department of Defense, September 2, 2014. As of May 9, 2016: http://archive.defense.gov/news/newsarticle.aspx?id=123059

Saferworld, *Mogadishu Rising? Conflict and Governance Dynamics in the Somali Capital*, London, August 2012.

"Shabaab Arrests Fighters Pledged to IS," SITE Intelligence Group, October 2015. As of May 9, 2016: https://ent.siteintelgroup.com/Jihadist-News/shabaab-arrests-fighters-pledged-to-is.html

"Shabaab Fighters' Pledges to IS Prompts Disputes Among Jihadists, Unanimous Prediction of Bloodshed," SITE Intelligence Group, October 2015.

Shil, Mohamed, "Al-Shabab: What Will Happen Next?" *Somalia Report*, September 3, 2011. As of May 9, 2016: http://www.somaliareport.com/index.php/post/194/Al-Shabab_What_Will_Happen_Next

Shy, John, and Thomas W. Collier, "Revolution War," in Peter Paret, ed., *Makers of Modern Strategy: From Machiavelli to the Nuclear Age*, Princeton, N.J.: Princeton University Press, 1986, pp. 815–862.

Simeone, Nick, "U.S. Conducts Counterterrorism Operations in Somalia," U.S. Department of Defense, March 13, 2015. As of May 9, 2016: http://www.defense.gov/News-Article-View/Article/604274

"Somalia Famine Killed Nearly 260,000 People, Half of Them Children, Reports UN," United Nations News Centre, May 2, 2013. As of July 6, 2016: http://www.un.org/apps/news/story.asp?NewsID=44811#.V32JYRUrJMA

"Somalia's Shabab Calls on Global Islamist Militants to Attack Ugandan and Burundian Targets," *Jane's Terrorism and Insurgency Centre*, July 9, 2010.

Somaliland Times, "Extremist Splinter Group of Somali Islamic Courts Formed," August 12, 2006.

Stewart, Christopher S., "A Bet on Peace for War-Torn Somalia," *Wall Street Journal*, April 26, 2013. As of May 9, 2016: http://www.wsj.com/articles/SB10001424127887323820304578410573747048086

UN—*See* United Nations.

United Nations, *The Blue Helmets: A Review of United Nations Peace-keeping*, 3rd ed., New York: UN Department of Public Information, 1996.

———, *Population Estimation Survey 2014: For the 18 Pre-War Regions of Somalia*, October 2014.

United Nations High Commissioner for Refugees, "Return to Somalia: No Longer a Refugee," August 7, 2015. As of May 9, 2016:
http://www.unhcr.org/55c517346.html

United Nations Security Council, "Resolution 1744," S/RES/1744, February 21, 2007.

———, "Resolution 2036," S/RES/2036, February 22, 2012.

United States Code, Title 50, Section 413, War and National Defense, amended April 21, 2005.

———, Title 50, Section 3001, National Security Act of 1947, sec. 503(e), enacted December 18, 2015.

United States District Court for the District of Minnesota, *United States of America v. Mohamed Abdihamid Farah, Adnan Abdihamid Farah, Abdurahman Yasin Daud, Zacharia Yusuf Abdurahman, Hanad Mustafe Musse, and Guled Ali Omar*, Criminal Complaint, April 18, 2015.

United States District Court, District of New Jersey, *United States of America v. Mohamed Alessa and Carlos E. Almonte*, Magistrate No.: 10-8109 (MCA), June 4, 2010. As of May 9, 2016:
https://www.justice.gov/archive/usao/nj/Press/files/pdffiles/2010/Alessa,%20 Mohamed%20and%20Almonte,%20Carlos%20Complaint.pdf

United States District Court for the Eastern District of Virginia, Alexandria Division, *United States of America v. Zachary Adam Chesser*, Position of the United States with Respect to Sentencing Factors, Case 1:10-cr-00395-LO, Document 46, February 18, 2011. As of May 9, 2016:
http://www.investigativeproject.org/documents/case_docs/1486.pdf

U.S. Department of Defense, "Department of Defense Press Briefing by Rear Adm. Kirby in the Pentagon Briefing Room," News Transcript Press Operations, September 2, 2014a. As of May 9, 2016:
http://www.defense.gov/News/News-Transcripts/Transcript-View/Article/606923/ department-of-defense-press-briefing-by-rear-adm-kirby-in-the-pentagon-briefing

———, "Statement by Pentagon Press Secretary Rear Adm. John Kirby on Today's Airstrike in Somalia," Release No.: NR-633-14, December 29, 2014b. As of May 9, 2016:
http://www.defense.gov/News/News-Releases/News-Release-View/Article/605333

———, "Statement from Pentagon Press Secretary Peter Cook on December 2 Airstrike in Somalia," Release No: NR-462-15, Washington, D.C., December 7, 2015. As of May 9, 2016:
http://www.defense.gov/News/News-Releases/News-Release-View/Article/633220/statement-from-pentagon-press-secretary-peter-cook-on-dec-2-airstrike-in-somalia

———, "Statement from Pentagon Press Secretary Peter Cook on Airstrike in Somalia," Release No: NR-076-16, Washington, D.C., March 7, 2016. As of July 6, 2016:
http://www.defense.gov/News/News-Releases/News-Release-View/Article/687305/statement-from-pentagon-press-secretary-peter-cook-on-airstrike-in-somalia

U.S. Department of State, *Country Reports on Terrorism*, various years. As of May 9, 2016:
http://www.state.gov/j/ct/rls/crt/

———, *Country Reports on Terrorism 2005*, Washington, D.C. April 2006, p. 9.

U.S. Department of State, Office of the Coordinator for Counterterrorism, "Designation of al-Shabaab," March 18, 2008. As of May 9, 2016:
http://www.state.gov/j/ct/rls/other/des/143205.htm

"We Have a Terror Recruiting Problem in Minnesota," *CBS News*, April 20, 2015. As of May 9, 2016:
http://www.cbsnews.com/news/six-minnesota-men-arrested-trying-to-join-isis-identified/

Weber, Max, "Politics as a Vocation," in H. H. Gerth and C. Wright Mills, eds., *From Max Weber: Essays in Sociology*, New York: Oxford University Press, 1958, p. 78.

Whitlock, Craig, and Kevin Sieff, "U.S. Launches Drone Strike Against al Shabab Figure Tied to Kenya Mall Attack," *Washington Post*, March 13, 2015. As of May 9, 2016:
https://www.washingtonpost.com/world/national-security/us-launches-drone-strike-against-al-shabab-figure-tied-to-attack-on-kenya-mall/2015/03/13/c00086a0-c98b-11e4-a199-6cb5e63819d2_story.html

Wise, Rob, "Al-Shabaab," AQAM Future Project Case Studies Report, Washington, D.C.: Center for Strategic and International Studies, July 2011.

World Bank, "Data: Somalia," undated. As of October 12, 2015:
http://data.worldbank.org/country/somalia

Yusuf, Mohammed, "Poll: Eight in 10 Kenyans See Al-Shabab as 'Major Threat,'" *Voice of America*, April 17, 2015. As of May 9, 2016:
http://www.voanews.com/content/ipsos-poll-kenya-al-shabab/2723877.html

Index

See also individual operations
terrorism
  defined, 5
  following September 11, 2001, 38
Terrorism Events Database, 65
terrorist attacks
  increasing violence of, 29
  in Kenya, 23
terrorist group(s)/organization(s)
  al Shabaab designated by U.S. as, 16
  extremist narrative of, 35
  shift of al Shabaab from insurgent group to, 29
  territorial control for, 42
TFG. *See* Transitional Federal Government
Thornton, Richard T., 52
Tiyeeglow district, 44
training
  augmenting, 60
  from United States, 47–48
Transitional Federal Government (TFG)
  AMISOM support of, 14
  illegitimacy of, 14–15
  in Mogadishu, 13–14
  Operation Linda Nchi, 23
  territorial gains in 2013, 26
  territorial victories in retreat and adaptation phase, 23
  in war with clan-based militias, 15
TTP (Tehreek-e-Taliban Pakistan), 41

Uganda
  challenges for, 61
  role in countering al Shabaab, 60–61
  sanctuary for al Shabaab operatives in, 26
Ugandan embassies, al Shabaab's encouragement of attacks on, 20
Ugandan forces
  in AMISOM forces' clearing of Mogadishu, 43
  Operation Indian Ocean, 44, 45

retake of Lower and Middle Shabelle territory, 44
Unified Task Force (UNITAF)
  in Somalia, 1992 to 1995, 10
  transition to UNOSOM II by, 37
  U.S. forces in, 36–37
United Kingdom, aid and training from, 46
United Nations Operation in Somalia I (UNOSOM I), 10
United Nations Operation in Somalia II (UNOSOM II)
  in Somalia, 1992 to 1995, 10
  transition from UNITAF to, 37
  U.S. forces in, 36
United Nations Political Office for Somalia, 53
United States
  aid to AMISOM and Somalia's neighbors, 60–61
  al Shabaab as threat to, 1
  al Shabaab recruits from, 15
  in coalition cooperating against extremists, 48
  counterterrorism campaign, 11–12
  deadline for withdrawal from Somalia, 38
  increasing economic assistance from, 59–60
  information collection by, 48
  as perceived enemy of al Shabaab, 2–3, 35
  policy recommendations for, 59–62
  resources committed by, 62
  robust intervention, 36–39, 54
  support to al Shabaab opponents, 46–51
  tailored engagement by, 39–51
  tailored engagement strategy, 54
  training, advice, and assistance from, 47–48, 60
United States forces
  direct action by, 48–51, 61–62
  indirect engagement by, 34–35, 54–55
  in Iraq, 38